To Joanna

The Lutterworth Press
P.O. Box 60
Cambridge
CB1 2NT

British Library Cataloguing-in-Publication Data
A catalogue record for this book is available from the British Library

ISBN 0-7188-2863-1

Copyright © Philip Blair 1993

First published by The Lutterworth Press 1993

Printed in Great Britain by
Hillman Printers (Frome) Ltd.

Contents

Preface

Today's Church has embraced the world.

The spectacle confronting us is that of a Church involving herself in the full range of human activities, not just indirectly through her members, who are also members of a wider society, but directly, in her corporate capacity. Indeed, we see the gospel narratives being reinterpreted in such a way that authority for this direct involvement is claimed from the founder of Christianity himself.

The cry is that we can no longer distinguish between the spiritual and the political. Sermons, books, reports, and articles almost all nowadays take this point for granted. Those who query it are brushed aside as simple-minded pietists who, in rejecting worldliness, are insufficiently concerned about the material needs of those around them and wrongly dismissive of an overriding Christian obligation to change the structures of society in the interests of a more egalitarian world.

In our materialistic times this new gospel has a certain plausibility, expounded as it is by countless professional churchmen or theologians. With such, however, I would take issue. For I have sought (in Africa and the Middle East, as much as in England) to witness to the truth of Christ's Gospel, and have found the ubiquitous 'church political' to be a constant encumbrance. More to the point is the fact that I have discovered nothing in the New Testament which gives sanction for politicization of the Gospel.

The problem with politics is that it is all about moralizing. One ideology or group of people is commended, another is condemned. Everybody loves moralizing, so occasionally the Church is applauded for acting the moral tutor. What results more often, however, is the alienation of those to whom the Church is supposed to be offering not (at best) a pep-talk, nor (at worst) a slating, but the loving invitation to a new kind of life altogether through the Christ who never condemned sinners.

The message of Jesus is, in fact, a transcendent one. Or, as Arnold Toynbee once expressed it, Christianity is a religion of transfiguration. It is one that defines salvation neither in terms of economic and political materialism, nor in terms of complete detachment, but rather in terms of the spiritual regeneration of the individual who must then both witness to and work in a fallen world. This true Christian perspective, indicating the

v

real nature of the Church and her Gospel, contrasts fundamentally both with the world-affirming optimism that leads to compromise with worldly power, and with the world-denying pessimism that entails an abrogation of genuine responsibilities.

The Church was appointed to be the single custodian and teacher of a new and distinctive revelation about man's potential in Christ, and it is this task which she is compromising - and even at times abandoning - by entering the political arena. She does not, by doing so, help society, as invariably she bases her political arguments on premises appropriate only for life lived within the Christian community, and in this way she certainly does not add to her own numbers. Her conduct is therefore doubly to be censured in practice, as well as being utterly wrong in principle.

Having stated my case in embryo, I argue it more comprehensively in the following pages. I do so, in Part I, by tracing the history of the Church through a period of almost two thousand years, a period during which the Church has oscillated between faithfulness and apostasy. In particular, I show how the truth has at times been almost totally obscured, needing to be proclaimed afresh. In Part II, I examine Christian origins in order to identify the nature of the Church and her Gospel. I conclude by examining the Christian's proper relationship to the secular sphere.

I make no claims for this being an original book, although it may well appear controversial to some. It is simply a restatement of the view that was delivered to us by Christ, expounded by St Paul, perceived by St Francis, protested by Luther, presupposed by Wesley - and has been discarded. It is an attempt to redress what I believe to be a serious imbalance in the thinking of almost all modern Christians.

Finally, for advice on and assistance with the text of this work I would like to thank David Bolt, my agent, Colin Lester and Richard Burnell of The Lutterworth Press, and my son, Edmund. My family as a whole are to be thanked for their patience and encouragement, and my friend Ann Morley for attending to the excellent Index.

Biblical quotations, unless otherwise stated, are from the Revised Standard Version.

Philip Blair

Muscat, October 1992

Part I
Wheat and Chaff

1

A Violent End, a Quiet Beginning

Zealotry: origins and development

The Jewish war with Rome,[1] which raged across Palestine for nearly eight years in the seventh and eighth decades of the first century of the Christian era, was no sudden or unexpected event. It had long been been brewing in the underground cellars of Jewish Zealotry.

The movement of Jewish resistance to Rome, to which we can loosely give the epithet 'Zealotry', was effectively born in AD 6, when there was a surge of popular opposition to the census mounted by the Romans in Judaea for tax purposes. This act of resistance, the details of which are somewhat obscure, was led by one Judas, called the Galilean, who was perhaps the focal point of a discontent of even longer standing.[2] Judas and his followers opposed the payment of tribute by Israel to a pagan on the ground that this was treason to God, Israel's true and only king; in this way they showed conspicuous zeal for the Law - a zeal that matched that of the Maccabean Jews before them and the zealous Phinehas before that, in what were regarded as times of religious apostasy. The views held and propagated by Judas, with the support of a Pharisee named Saddock, were described by the Jewish historian Josephus as the 'fourth philosophy' among the Jews, the other three being those of the Pharisees, Sadducees and the Essenes.[3]

It seems that Judas himself perished in or shortly after the uprising he fomented, but though many of his followers were either killed or scattered his two sons, James and Simon (later to be crucified by Tiberius Alexander), took over the task of disseminating their father's teaching and of keeping the spirit of resistance alive. In this they were wholly successful. Jesus of Nazareth, it seems clear, was tempted to become a political leader. The issue of revolt against Rome still burned strongly and Jesus might well have been the outstanding leader that the Zealots needed. Indeed, the whole East might easily have risen to follow the lead of someone who by a quick success revealed himself capable of seriously challenging Rome's occupation of one of her more far-flung provinces. Suetonius tells us that it was from Judaea that the East expected the deliverer from Roman dominion to come.[4]

Jesus, however, was crucified by the Roman governor of Judaea - who feared to do anything that might incite a hostile Jewish populace, hugely swollen at Passover time, to violence. Pontius Pilate had already acquired a

3

reputation for antagonizing the Jews, and it was only a few years after the death of Jesus that he finally overreached himself by executing the leaders of a group of Samaritans who had gathered at Mount Gerizim at the call of a pretender. Pilate was recalled to Rome to answer before the Emperor charges brought against him by the Samaritans.

But Pilate's recall did nothing to calm the rising storm of passion that rocked the Jewish world in the years following the death of Jesus. Nor did the subsequent despatch from Rome of a rapid succession of procurators alleviate a situation degenerating into chaos. The spirit of riot was released with fearful violence as rival factions strove with one another for ascendancy. Bands of brigands, who operated with the organized techniques of modern criminals, systematically plundered the large estate owners on the pretext of obtaining funds for their factional campaigns. Economic conditions deteriorated dramatically, and unemployment was rife. Messianic extremism combined with gangsterism in inciting the masses to disorder, while the occupying Roman forces encouraged both, in their effects, by obscenely insulting the Jews' sacred institutions.

As disaffection and lawlessness spread, the Temple at Jerusalem was increasingly regarded by the Romans as the symbolic focus of the disorders. At the annual Feasts of the Passover and of Tabernacles, to which as many as three million Jews from the provinces would flock[5], visitors became the dupes of disappointed agitators and Zealots, as well as the prey of rogues, until the Feasts eventually became the chief occasions of outbreaks of violence, murder, and even massacre, and the Temple the centre of the tumults.

In AD 40 the Romans perpetrated the grossest outrage of all. In the spring of that year the Jews demolished at Jamnia an altar newly erected in honour of Gaius Caligula to mark his German victories. Incensed that the Jews refused to pay him the divine honours he believed to be his due, Caligula ordered a colossal statue of himself, asserting his divinity, to be constructed and positioned inside the Temple at Jerusalem. Petronius, the governor of Syria, was to implement this, and he personally led an army to Jerusalem to carry it out. On his way, however, he was confronted by great numbers of the Jewish populace who said they were 'ready to expose themselves, together with their children and wives, to be slain' rather than let an image of Caesar be placed in the Temple.[6] Petronius was finally persuaded to put his own life at risk by discontinuing the attempt of his own volition. He would, indeed, have forfeited his life had not news of the death of the Emperor reached him before Caligula's own message ordering his death.[7]

So progressed the sequence of riot and disorder, of Roman provocation and Jewish resistance, active and passive, of tumults and rumours of wars and all the social and economic unrest already described that accompanies the breakdown of political order. Josephus, indeed, almost makes it seem that the war started some fifteen years before its true beginning when he writes that 'under Cumanus began the troubles, and the Jews' ruin came on'.[8] He proceeds to describe a variety of calamities: riots following the obscene insult of a Roman soldier, more riots following a 'tumult by robbers' in which further blasphemous provocation was offered by the Roman soldiery, fights in Samaria leading to a massacre of Samaritans by a Jewish mob led by one Eleazer, a pseudo-patriot and arch-gangster, who with his associated band of ruffians had plundered the country for twenty years following the fall of Pontius Pilate. Cumanus came to the assistance of the beleaguered Samaritans, slaying great numbers of Eleazer's followers. Meanwhile the rulers of Jerusalem prevailed upon their fellow Jews who had gone out to plunder the Samaritans to disperse, though, Josephus adds, 'still there were a great number who betook themselves to robbing, in hopes of impunity, and rapines and insurrections of the bolder sort happened over the whole of the country'.[9]

These disturbances led to the recall and subsequent banishment of Cumanus, in whose place as procurator Antonius Felix was appointed. He captured Eleazer and many others and sent them to Rome, also crucifying an untold number of robbers and their accomplices. This only left the field clear for an even worse form of bandit to appear in the form of the Sicarii, 'who slew men in the daytime, and in the midst of the city ... chiefly at the festivals, when they mingled themselves among the multitude, and concealed daggers under their garments, with which they stabbed those that were their enemies; and when any fell down dead, the murderers became a part of those that had indignation against them, by which means . . . they could by no means be discovered. The first man who was slain by them was Jonathan the high priest, after whose death many were slain every day . . .'. At the same time, false prophets, claiming divine inspiration, abounded, the most notorious being an Egyptian who, with thirty thousand men, planned to break into Jerusalem from the Mount of Olives.[10]

The whole situation spiralled downwards in such confusion that, when one disturbance was quietened, 'it happened', Josephus writes, 'as it does in a diseased body, that another part was subject to an inflammation . . . till all Judaea was filled with the effects of ... madness. And thus the flame was every day more and more blown up, till it came to a direct war'.[11]

And yet that direct war was delayed in its coming for year after year. The procurator Festus succeeded Felix, and Festus was displaced by Florus, who finally provoked the Jews to the unpardonable act that precipitated the war. This was the massacre of the Roman garrison in Jerusalem and setting fire to the citadel on the seventeenth day of the Jewish month Ab, AD 66.[12] It had almost occurred three months earlier; indeed on first reading it seems that Josephus thus dated the final outbreak of hostilities. But these earlier outbreaks were brought to an end on the appeal of King Agrippa, and it appears to have been after further repeated acts of provocation by Florus, 'because his design was to have a war kindled', that the Jews committed the act of no return. It followed the persuasion of those that officiated in the Divine Service by Eleazer, son of the high priest, to receive no gift or sacrifice from a foreigner. This, Josephus concludes, 'was the true beginning of our war with the Romans; for they rejected the sacrifice of Caesar on this account'.[13]

A fearful climax

Josephus' account of the war, in which he himself played a part, makes fascinating, if horrific, reading. He traces the Jews' early successes, then the conquest of Samaria, Peraea, Idumaea and the coastal region of Judaea under Vespasian in AD 68, then the year's delay in operations until Vespasian's command had been confirmed following Nero's suicide, then the transference of the command to Titus in AD 69, who, after encountering long delays in Alexandria and Caesarea, only really began operations in the spring of AD 70, then, finally, the fearful climax in the summer of that year, when Jerusalem fell to Titus' army. Not that the war ended even then, for Josephus traces how the struggle in Palestine continued with unabated fury for over three years, and how it was prolonged almost indefinitely in adjacent provinces of the Roman Empire.

The siege itself was of relatively short duration. It commenced at the Feast of the Passover, AD 70, when multitudes from the provinces had crowded into Jerusalem only to find themselves suddenly imprisoned, when the Romans, having hovered nearby in their encircling strongholds for two years, chose that moment to descend and invest the city. Of the conditions inside the city, when pestilence broke out, closely followed by famine, when on top of this the rule of terrorism prevailed, faction fighting with faction for dominance, agreeing only in arms when fanatically resisting and attacking the Romans,[14] Josephus can scarcely find words fittingly terrible. 'Thus did the miseries of Jerusalem grow worse and worse every day, and the seditious were still more irritated by the calamities they were under, even while the famine preyed upon themselves, after it had preyed upon the people, and indeed the multitude of carcases that lay in heaps upon another, was an horrible sight, and produced a pestilential stench, which was an hinderance to those that would make sallies out of the city, and fight the enemy . . .'.[15] 'Accordingly', he concludes, 'the multitude of those that therein perished, exceeded all the destructions that either men or God ever brought upon the world . . .'[16] According to Josephus, well over a million perished in the city during the siege, and he records that out of one gate only of the city were passed in the night 115,880 corpses in the seventy-six days from the arrival of the Romans on the first day of the month Tammuz.[17]

Such figures, and such catastrophes, are all too tragically familiar to the twentieth century reader, even as he reclines in the comfort of an armchair. Though perhaps it is the chaos and terror of disharmony within, when men's hands are raised against their own brothers, that strikes the most sickeningly familiar chord for us today.

Arnold Toynbee once wrote the following: 'In the face of an external menace, the human spirit can find relief in either endurance or action. The onslaught of an overwhelmingly stronger human enemy can be resisted to the death; an act of God can be accepted with resignation; but when we feel that "we are betrayed by that which is false within" we are apt to find ourselves spiritually paralysed in the face of the most deadly peril with which humanity is ever confronted.'[18] This tissue of mutual distrust between factions, between parties, between classes, proved to be a deadly peril for the Jews when the conflagration came in the form of a war amongst themselves as well as against Rome.

Another way

Yet at the very moment of catastrophe a single incident may sometimes point the true way forward. It was perhaps in realization of the ultimate folly of turning upon your own kindred and nation, if not the folly of challenging any lawful authority with violence, that led one Jewish Rabbi, Johanan ben Zakkai, to believe that the war against Rome had been a mistake. He believed that the Jews must live by the spirit, not the sword, and it is of him that our incident speaks. As the moment of supreme disaster for Jerusalem approached, Johanan arranged with his disciples to be carried out of the walls as one dead and ready for burial. Brought miraculously beyond the lines of danger, Johanan, an old man, arose from his coffin and made his way to Vespasian.[19] There, in that simple confrontation, and for a brief moment, was enacted again the drama of the meeting of the two extremes of polarity, as with Jesus before Pilate, St Francis before the Sultan, Luther before the Emperor - and the list could be extended. Like many others, Johanan risked his life in the interests of a kingdom he, like that other Rabbi forty years before, had learnt was 'not of this world.'[20] For that kingdom one could not fight.

Johanan's life was spared by Vespasian, and his request to set up a school in the little seaside town of Jabne (or Jamnia) was granted. From these unlikely beginnings a new, and necessarily more spiritual, form of Judaism was born.

After the fall of Jerusalem there could be no more Temple sacrifices, but the sacrifice of prayer could go on. It was Hosea, not Jesus, who first said 'I desire mercy, and not sacrifice'.[21]

Sadly, the lessons taught by Rabbi Johanan were not widely heeded at first. They were not heeded sufficiently to prevent a second country-wide revolt in Judaea between the years AD 132-5, led by one Simeon Bar Kochba. It was only after this revolt had been crushed, again with great loss of life, that the new way which Johanan had first pointed to became generally accepted. But by that time what had once seemed no more than a sect of the Jews, the Christian sect, was surging ahead - albeit below the surface of the world's political events.

2
Commitment, Compromise and the Crusades

A spiritual conquest

It has been disputed that Jesus, and the early Christians, especially the early Jewish Christians, kept themselves clear of the violent revolutionary movement represented by Zealotry.[1] The main lines of evidence, however, indicate that Jesus and - after his death - the first Christians considered such revolution wrong, and refused to support it.[2] One need not quibble, of course, about the possibility of a few isolated Christians having been implicated in a revolt like the first century Jewish revolt. But such people, if they existed - and there is no hard evidence to suggest that they did - would have been exceptional. The Christian rule from the very beginning appears to have been one of non-involvement in such conflicts. At all events, with regard to the Jewish War, two early Christian authorities state that at around the time of the outbreak of hostilities in AD 66 the Christians of Judaea left Jerusalem, having been divinely guided to do so. Whatever impelled them to leave (and Jesus' own warnings must have been a factor), they apparently crossed the Jordan and took refuge in Pella.[3]

Not that Christians eschewed the duties of citizenship, even accepting the role of public servants, actively assisting in the running of society under the State authorities.[4] It was binding upon all Christians to be good citizens, whereas resisting the demands of the State, unless these were incompatible with a Christian's loyalty to God, or undermining the structure of society by violent means, were actions expressly forbidden.[5] To the Christian, as to the Rabbi Johanan, the Kingdom of God of which he was a member was 'not of this world'.[6]

If, however, the early Christians were not guilty of sedition, beyond their membership of a body that might be traduced as an illegal and politically motivated 'guild' because of its members' refusal to uphold the State religion,[7] they cannot have lacked temptations to err in that direction. The use of violence to gain Jewish national independence was a temptation at the beginning, for it is unquestionable that during his lifetime Jesus' followers misunderstood his intentions, tending to assume that his aim was that of a seizure of worldly power.[8] Once Jesus had left them, however, the Christians understood that they were not to work for the establishment of an earthly kingdom, but that their distinctive mission was to be one of witnessing to the spiritual truths he had taught them.[9]

The Christians' temptation to compromise came, therefore, not because of a lingering desire to further Jewish national aspirations (more and more Gentiles were becoming Christians, in any case), but because of the periods of savage persecution directed against them at an official level by the Roman authorities. There was the temptation to avoid death, and probably a hideous one, by burning incense to the Emperor, or by offering meat to be roasted on a fire in the name of a pagan divinity and then consumed. Of those, probably a minority of professing Christians, who were actually faced with this stark choice, not a few succumbed. In so doing they denied exclusive spiritual sovereignty to Jesus, the Church's one Lord - only to suffer the strongest condemnation by their confessing brethren and church leaders (though some bishops also lapsed, or hid). But there must also have been, for some at least, the temptation to join in with acts of violent resistance against an authority itself cruelly violent towards certain of its subjects. When, indeed, the pogroms against Christians took place, as under Decius in the third century, against a background of political troubles within the Empire, such a temptation must have been especially real. Yet throughout that century - whilst civil discord grew with the lowering of morale from the Senate downwards, whilst alien immigration and alien manning of the legions accelerated with the falling of the Roman birth-rate, whilst the frontiers were ever more heavily threatened and there were clashes even within the Empire between rival emperors and rival armies - the Christians were conspicuous by their studied avoidance, apart from their refusal to worship the Emperor or his gods, of anything that might savour of civil disobedience.

Up to the conversion of Constantine early in the fourth century 'the spread of Christianity,' writes Herbert Butterfield, 'from that narrow and unpromising region where it had its birth, over the length and breadth of the civilized world, is one of the most moving stories that history has to offer us - one of the clearest cases ever known of the meek inheriting the earth. Islam was to be very different - it was to extend itself by military conquest. No one could accuse the followers of Christ of having made it their object, in the first three centuries, even to capture the Roman government.'[10]

Worldly compromise

With the conversion of Constantine the story took a different turn. Christianity was legalized; then it became fashionable; once fashionable, it was open to corruption and compromise - flirtation with the world. Expediency rather than principle began to govern its behaviour and mould its character. Indeed, right up to the time of the Reformation, the Western Church increasingly assumed the character of a political power in her own right. Herbert

Butterfield, in fact, sees no fundamental change in this aspect of the Church's character even at the Reformation: 'In spite of the set-back a little later under Julian, the conversion of Constantine opened a period which hardly ended until the twentieth century - a period in which the religion of the New Testament was to have the alliance of power, and was to be now the support, now the agent, now the suffering colleague, and now the passive accomplice of secular authority.'[11]

This involvement of the Western Church in the political sphere never quite reached the fusion of spiritual and temporal powers, the Caesaro-Papism, which was the lot of the Eastern Empire for a thousand years after the Barbarian invasions. Those very invasions, which the alliance between the Church and the government in the fourth century was powerless to avert, 'saved' the Western Empire from the theocratic ideal, although attempts were later made to realize it. In the fifth century, government, society and Roman civilization itself faced disaster, the trauma of conquest leading to general instability and cultural decline following the first and then successive invasions and migrations. This state of affairs continued for five hundred years. It was in this political vacuum that the Western Church, the Papacy, consolidated its political power.

Rome was overwhelmed three times between AD 410 and 476. The first devastation, in AD 410, was at the hands of Alaric and the Goths. Some four decades later, in AD 453, only humiliating terms obtained from Attila and the Huns saved the city; Leo the Great, Bishop of Rome, was to a large extent responsible for this reprieve. Rome was overwhelmed a second time, however, by Genseric the Vandal, who, sailing from Carthage gained control of the mouth of the Tiber and completely ransacked the city. Leo again intervened, saving many lives as a result, though failing to stop the pillage and destruction. But Italy was by then in a state of anarchy, with Barbarian chiefs competing for power. Rome was finally overrun by the forces of Ricimer the Sueve, theoretically the general of a confederation of Barbarian armies which governed what was left of Imperial Rome. Ricimer's succession of nominees to the imperial throne were in turn unable to consolidate their position, until the penultimate one, Anthemius, refusing to defer to his patron and thereby incurring his wrath, was attacked by him in Rome. The 'eternal city' was thus devastated for the third time. The Empire finally collapsed in AD 476.

From the first years of the fifth century the government had been under two emperors, one at Rome, the other at Constantinople. The Eastern Empire, as we have seen, remained for centuries with the Emperor head of Church as well as State. The West, however, was left without a supreme authority to whom people could appeal - apart from the head of the Church. More and more appeals came to be made to the Bishop of Rome - the Pope. From AD 590, under Gregory the Great, the Papacy's power was immensely extended. Nominally he was a subject of Maurice, the Eastern Emperor; in practice he ruled Italy. He made treaties with the Lombards, who were the current threat; he averted yet another attack on Rome; he held negotiations with the Franks in Gaul; he acquired and controlled large estates in many foreign countries. In all, we see at this time the emergence of a second, European Christendom. Indeed, we see the genesis of Europe as we know it today.

Despite the hand that the Church had in its shaping, the formation of 'Christian' Europe was by no means a pacific affair. Whilst Pope Gregory used the monasteries as strategic centres for the spread of Roman Christianity, there were other more militant forms of missionary work going on.

All this time, and for centuries longer, the Barbarians, Teutonic peoples and dynasties, were continuing to overrun France, Spain, Italy and Britain. Some of these people were already Christian. Those who were not, or who were adherents of an Arian form of the faith, found it politic to adopt orthodox Roman Christianity. These semi-converted Barbarians then took upon themselves a missionary role - only sometimes it was evangelism at the point of a sword, as when Charlemagne subdued the Saxons, or, later, when the Germans conquered and colonized across the Elbe in the lands of the primitive Slavs. European monarchs often adopted Christianity for political reasons, and when their subjects did not spontaneously follow their example some monarchs compelled their people to be baptized. There ensued, in some instances, as in Hungary, terrible civil wars.

In all this the Church found a wonderfully fluid situation in which she was able to consolidate her position of influence and authority in the political sphere. And it is in respect of this, her role as a secular power - to the extent even of raising armies for the defence or extension of the Kingdom of God which she claimed to be serving - that it becomes impossible not to make a direct comparison with that other successful and concurrently expanding religion, Islam. For Muslims, of course, the concept of *jihad*, or Holy War, is intrinsic to the Qur'anic faith, as is the theocratic ideal; by mounting the Crusades, as well as by her more general political stance, the Church, without analogous support from her own Holy Book, sought to interpret Christianity in similar terms.

The bloody Crusades: the Church's 'holy war'
'Brought together from every nationality and generation, they came to the East with hearts filled with hatred and blood dripping from their hands.' They had come, 'to cut the throats of the Muslims.' So writes, of the Crusades, a modern Muslim apologist.[12] Since the armies of the Crusades were recruited by the Church and marched under the sign of the cross, the Muslim can be pardoned for failing to recognize the true Christian mission. When the same Muslim apologist can, with justification, go on to write that the Crusaders 'slashed in their progress even the throats of Christians who did not respond to their preaching, differed in opinion, or belonged to Christian sects other

than theirs',[13] it is even more tragically apparent what a grotesque distortion of Christ's religion had taken place under the Church's own hand. More moderate Muslim writers may emphasize that there was faith, principle and heroism behind some of the Crusaders' actions, or point to the economic, social and political pressures that were involved.[14] The fact remains that the Crusades represent a blatant forsaking by the Church of her true Christian mission in favour of crude power politics. The legacy of mistrust and resentment those armies bequeathed has never been wholly eradicated.[15]

The dates most usually cited as marking the beginning and ending of the period of the Crusades are 1095 and 1291. On 27 November 1095, Pope Urban II formally and solemnly declared the Crusade in his speech to the Church hierarchy and the French nobility in the Council of Clermont-Ferrand in the Auvergne. He was, in fact, only giving official voice to what had been germinating as an idea at the Papal Curia under his predecessor, Pope Gregory VII, the famous Hildebrand. When, in 1071, the battle of Manzikert showed up the vulnerability of the Byzantine Empire, Christianity's bulwark in the East against the Turks, it became plain that direct action would be needed to save the Christian East from being overrun. To Gregory's concern to save the Eastern Empire, Urban added the deliverance of Jerusalem and the surrounding Holy Places. Neither Urban, nor other preachers of the Crusades like Peter the Hermit, and, later, Bernard of Clairvaux, who thrilled Europe's princes and peasants with the call to acquire merit by fighting righteous wars, included among the motives for marching the conversion of Muslims. Rather did they dwell upon the sufferings of Christians in the East and the defilement of the Holy Places by the infidel, who must be put to rout by the sword. The way of Christian pilgrims to the East must also be kept open. This was a further incentive to the Crusader, who would himself, as would all who came after him, earn a double grace by visiting the most sacred of all goals of pilgrimage.

So the Crusades took their course over the period of two centuries, the balance of power swinging backwards and forwards between Christians and Muslims. Jerusalem, that fulcrum of so many of the world's worst conflicts, remained the ultimate prize even though the fiercest fighting was by no means reserved for her alone. In June, 1099, the city first fell to the Crusaders, amidst dreadful carnage, and the Latin kingdom of Jerusalem was proclaimed. Its first custodian, Godfrey of Bouillon, accepted the title of 'Defender of the Holy Sepulchre'. Defend it he did, defeating the first renewed Muslim challenge, in the form of an Egyptian army, as promptly as the following month. Godfrey died, however, in July 1100, and was succeeded by Baldwin of Boulogne, who was crowned king of the new theocratic state on Christmas Day that same year. The Christian kingdom thereafter settled down to its relatively peaceful though never very secure existence, disturbed periodically by influxes of pilgrims, and gaining some military support from the new military orders of religion. These Orders combined the profession of monasticism with that of fighting the enemies of the cross. As such the Knights Templar, and the other great Order of the Hospitallers, or order of St John of Jerusalem, became two prime instruments in keeping alive the Crusading spirit. Notwithstanding these Orders, nor the calling of other Crusades from time to time, Jerusalem fell to the Muslims again in 1187.

In 1229 Jerusalem, together with Bethlehem and Nazareth and some other few territories which had been lost, was restored to the Christians by the terms of a generous treaty between Sultan al-Kamil Muhammad of Egypt and the enigmatic 'Infidel Emperor', Frederick II, a lover of learning which included Arabic and Arabic philosophy. This was little more than an interlude, however, and an unhappy one at that; the Christian kingdom was the scene of internal strife and only lasted as long as it did because of similar strife amongst the Muslims. It fell to the Muslims in 1244, and most of Palestine went the same way the following year. The tide had turned for the Crusaders; indeed the high point for the Christians had been reached a full century before, the fall of Edessa in 1144 marking the first eroding of the fullest extent of Christian conquest. A major Crusade was mounted against Egypt after the second fall of Jerusalem, but to little avail. Indeed, the original Crusading ideal had suffered severe diminution with the sack of Constantinople by Crusaders in 1204, the Albigensian Crusade of 1208 and the numerous European expeditions conducted against schismatics or heretics or any who in general antagonized the Popes. It was no wonder that the gathering strength of the Muslims led at last to the decisive seizure of Acre in 1291, and to the surrender of all the remaining Christian outposts the following year.

A *lone initiative*

One man in all this time of wasted effort and misapplied energy both saw the true way forward and gambled all he had - being nothing and everything - to initiate another kind of offensive.

St Francis, the poor man of Assisi, *le jongleur de Dieu* and His fool, joined the fifth Crusade as it was encamped in Egypt in 1219 and persuaded Pelagius of Albano, the Spanish cardinal legate in command, to allow him to cross over the battle line to the Sultan's camp and attempt his conversion to Christianity. Francis was convinced this was possible if the Gospel was presented in love and simplicity. It is said that he offered to undergo trial by ordeal in order to prove the truth of the Christ in whom he believed. The Sultan, al-Kamil Muhammad, was quite ready to listen with interest, and perhaps amusement, to this strange but obviously holy little man. Exactly what he made of St Francis and his message (he did not allow the trial by ordeal), the Sultan was sufficiently impressed, though unconverted, to order that the friar be unmolested as he freely returned to the Christian side.

Some have said that the Sultan considered St Francis insane, and so released him; others have emphasized the traditional courtesy with which the

Muslim will always receive a holy man; but surely it is G.K. Chesterton who is nearest to the truth. He writes of St Francis: 'Men liked him too much for himself to let him die for his faith; and the man was received instead of the message.' Francis' effort, Chesterton concludes, was 'like the beginnings of a great bridge that might have united East and West, and remains one of the great might-have-beens of history'.[16]

Perhaps it was not altogether a might-have-been (though St Francis apparently thought it was) if the saying is true: 'He who receives you receives me.'[17]

3
The Way of World Denial

In St Francis one may well see the most perfect expression of the desire, manifest from very early times in Christian history, to reject the growing worldliness which threatened the Church's life and to recover the first apostolic simplicity of the Gospel. It is unfortunate that few amongst those making this protest understood that Gospel as St Francis did. Too many rejected the world altogether, as well as worldliness, in their revolt against Christian compromise. The fact that others of them, like the Crusading Orders of Knights, illustrate a tendency for this world-rejecting movement to come full circle, and make the very compromise that their forerunners deplored, is one of the many ironies of history.

The early ascetics
The urge to asceticism and world-denial gained momentum in the Christian community as early as the second century. That it was not unknown even in New Testament times is clear from some of Paul's writings, though he shows little sympathy for ascetic exercises, including celibacy, conceived as necessary for spiritual growth.[1] But it was in the second century that we find individual Christians renouncing marriage and personal possessions in the attempt to walk more closely with God in prayer, as well as in works of mercy towards the needy.

At this stage such ascetics had no organized or communal way of life. They did not at first withdraw to live apart from the local congregation. They remained as a reminder to Christians of the transience of life and of the ultimate irrelevance of worldly possessions. As such, and as long as no suggestion was made that they had chosen the best way as against a second best way, they no doubt performed a useful service. Unfortunately, as the Church expanded rapidly in the third century, the idea gained ground that there was a double standard of Christian ethics - that of the ordinary Christian living in the world, and a loftier 'counsel of perfection' to which only the ascetic, through his celibacy in particular, could aspire. Gaining support and authority from the writings of Origen and Clement of Alexandria, the ascetics began increasingly to separate themselves and to live apart from ordinary congregations. At first they continued with their works of mercy, but the movement gradually became more and more individualistic and separatist.

Complete detachment from the world was coveted in a 'flight of the alone to the alone'. Martyrdom was the supreme goal.

Not surprisingly, this movement aroused the suspicion of the leaders of the normal congregational life of the Church. These, for the most part, were of course bishops. Their main worry was that the ascetics would pass beyond their control. The Egyptian deserts, and later those of Syria, were the favourite environments for many who chose complete detachment from the world to live as hermits. Such hermits were afforded the most intense respect and would from time to time be visited by pious individuals who sought from them an inspired word from the Lord. Implicit in the authority assumed by these hermits, and accepted by many Christians, was a threat to the wider consensus of Church authority as focused upon and wielded by the episcopacy.

Two fourth century Egyptian ascetics, Antony and Pachomius, serve well as specific examples; they indeed took matters a stage further.

Antony's life is known to us in detail from his biography written by St Athanasius, a profound admirer of the ascetic ideal. Indeed, Athanasius uses his subject as something of a voice for his own thoughts on the monastic vocation, thoughts strongly influenced by Greek philosophy. Antony himself, and the other early ascetics, did not share this influence; they were of the Coptic tradition. Antony's withdrawal from the world was a gradual process, beginning with the practice of asceticism in his own village, and culminating in twenty years of total solitude, 'battling with demons', in the desert. At the age of fifty-five he re-established contact with pilgrims, claiming authority as a teacher of asceticism, to which world renunciation a number were attracted.

Whilst Antony was the type for future solitaries, Pachomius was effectively progenitor of those who lived out the same ideal in community. Having received instruction in fasting, prayer and obedience from another holy man, with whom he worked for a living and gave away alms, he set up a community of ascetics in Southern Egypt by the Nile at a village called Tabennisi. Though Pachomius' monastery was not the first of a loosely-knit kind, it was the first in which monks lived in fellowship under a definite set of rules. In this it was 'to prove of unbounded significance for future ages'.[2]

Monastic communities and a role in society

The man who did most to ensure that the individualism and separatism of the early monks did not divide them from the life of the Church as a whole was Basil of Caesarea. He formulated the 'Rule of St Basil', to this day the basis of the rule followed in Eastern Christendom. In AD 358 he went to live as a hermit by the river Iris, near Neo-Caesarea, where he founded a monastery, and was joined by a few friends. In AD 370 he succeeded Eusebius as Bishop of Caesarea, but his rule was the basis of further communities he instituted in Asia Minor. It ensured that the authority of the local bishop was safeguarded.

In this way, Basil did more than avert a division amongst Christians; he questioned the assumption made by many that the monk was only pursuing his own salvation. He insisted, on the contrary, that a social aim must remain primary for the ascetic movement. This was in sharp contrast to the bizarre forms of asceticism practised by some, especially in Syria and Mesopotamia. In these regions there were ascetics who lived like animals on grass, or, like Symeon the Stylite (to whom even the great councils of the Church deferred, such was his prestige), domiciled on the top of a column.

The name of John Cassian must also be added to that of Basil as anticipating the normative form of monasticism which finally developed in both the Western and Eastern Churches. After a period as an ascetic in Palestine and Egypt, he moved to Constantinople, then to Rome, arriving finally, in AD 415, in Marseilles. Here he organized monastic communities of men and women after Eastern models. For Cassian the ideal was a life lived in solitude, in which alone the true end of asceticism could be pursued - a pure communion with God in prayer. This basic practicality of approach in some ways anticipated the achievement of Benedict, who was to lend his name to the form of monasticism that dominated the Western Church for centuries.

St Benedict formulated his Rule in the sixth century. The key-notes were simplicity and discipline, with a careful avoidance of the extremes of Eastern asceticism. 'The good sense of the West,' H.A.L. Fisher writes, 'avoided the eccentricities of the Egyptian solitary who, perched upon a pillar or a tree, exhibited the charms of his pious emaciation and squalor to the admiring pilgrim. The Latin genius was more practical, less speculative than the Greek.' [3] Benedict's practicality is above all exemplified in his requirement that monks should spend certain hours each day in manual labour. This led to something of an agricultural revival in the West, while from another injunction, that of intellectual study, stemmed the scholastic and cultural legacy that the Western world owes to the monastic movement.

Yet the social and cultural benefits that flowed from the proliferation of Benedictine communities remained largely a by-product of the still undenied aim of establishing a Christian enclave detached from society. The inspiration of the movement remained the rejection of worldliness: to be a monk constituted the surest way to heaven in a troubled world. To enter a monastery was to withdraw; there was no conscious intention to return to serve the wider Church or the world.

The pressure upon the religious Orders to become an active force in the world came from outside. Once the monastic movement was under the control of the bishops - the outcome for which Basil had successfully striven - the way was open for worldly-minded prelates to use the monks as a fighting force. Thus, in Egypt, the successors of Athanasius found in their monks a ready weapon for the destruction of pagan temples, or the combating of heresy, and in the West there developed the Crusading Orders of Knights. But other forces also contributed to a secularization of the monasteries, forces inherent in the society of the times.

The problem of recruitment was one to which Benedict devoted considerable attention. He envisaged three types of recruits: older laymen, clergy, and the children of noblemen. While the first two were expected to provide the bulk of aspiring members, the latter became increasingly common once the motive for entering had been modified to fulfil a social function. For, firstly, the monks were now being seen as special intercessors for the 'ordinary' Christian's temporal safety and eternal salvation. They had the time to pray and fast, sing elaborate rituals, and, above all, to say the Masses upon which the spiritual welfare of others was believed to depend. They could also expiate spiritual debt by performing those penances that the Church liberally imposed on lay-Christians. Thus rich men of the world became founders and benefactors of monasteries, or paid to have the monks fulfil their penitential obligations. Secondly, aristocratic families were finding in the rich and cultured monasteries homes for those of their children whom they could not adequately support in the secular world. A community so favoured would usually find itself the recipient of a handsome gift, usually of land, in return for which the donor would expect the monastery's co-operation in the work of government, especially in time of war.

Such were the influences that wrought a complete change in a monastic movement born of the desire to flee the world and opt out of society. Five centuries after Benedict, monks had become an indispensible cog in the machinery of society. Life, of course, was considered to be a unity. There were two modes of living, the religious and the secular, within one divinely ordered commonwealth. The religious, the monk, worked his passage in society, but within a microcosm of God's overall kingdom; in that microcosm the kingdom's features were most perfectly expressed, and the battle with a supernatural enemy fought out at the closest quarters. The secular man, engaged in the same battle, was free (freed, indeed, by the monk) to wage war at a lower, more mundane, level. Even this distinction was to become blurred as rulers increasingly used monasteries as centres of education and learning, appointing their abbots (as they appointed bishops), who then became state advisers and officials.

Serving King and Vicar: reaction and expansion
The whole of the Carolingian renaissance under Charlemagne, who was crowned Holy Roman Emperor in AD 800, was dependent upon the learning of the Church. Charlemagne, whose first adviser in educational matters was Alcuin, the English scholar, who later became Abbot of Tours, issued capitularies to the effect that teaching and study should go on in the schools of bishops, abbots, and even in local parishes. For the princely feudal bishops this was a new emphasis; for the parish priests it was almost impossible to

fulfil; for the monasteries it was only what they should already have been pursuing, in adherence to their Rule. Now, however, being dominated by great feudal families, the monasteries had become lax. Charlemagne tried to organize them under himself, removing from all except four the right to elect their own abbot.

A theocratic vision lay behind Carolingian Europe - the vision of a Church dominated by the Emperor, a 'Holy Roman Empire', claiming descent from Imperial Rome, governed, guarded and extended under the Emperor's divinely given authority through his princes and bishops. Education and centralization were the two indispensable keys. Whilst the monasteries already deferred to the one, they should be made to defer to the other. They should play their part, too, in the Christianizing of conquered territories like Saxony, where conversion had been enforced by savage enactments.

The vision ultimately faded. Charlemagne's attempt to dominate the monasteries and to make them permanent centres of learning met with two obstacles: the reforming zeal of a latter-day Benedict, for whom the life of education and culture was a denial of the ascetic ideal, and a little later the disturbance of the monasteries by Scandinavian raiders. Later still, with the waning of the power of the Carolingian kings, largely through loss of wealth, the Carolingian church order proved impracticable. The king was unable to support his bishops, whose power derived from him. The bishops therefore looked to the Papacy, and by the eleventh century the Church, under Gregory VII, had reclaimed the right to appoint them. As by this time the bishops were often wielding authority over secular rulers, the Papacy's temporal power was correspondingly enhanced.

Gregory VII, elected in 1073, brought the Papacy's political power to its maturity. Inspired by the ideals of the abbey of Cluny, the glorious apogee of Benedictine monasticism, he was zealous for widespread reform. His zeal, however, brought him into conflict with the Empire over supremacy in world politics; his concept of society was of a divinely governed state, such as Charlemagne had sought to create, but whose supreme head was not the king but Christ's vicar, the Papal successors to St Peter. In her new strength the Church, under Gregory, became embroiled in a power struggle with the Emperor on this issue. But as she did so there were renewed calls for a renunciation of worldliness and a return to the apostolic Gospel.

The new Orders of the Cistercians, the Carthusians and the Augustinians came into existence, along with some lesser lights, in the half century between 1075 and 1125. While the Carthusian Order, strictest of the three, did not proliferate greatly, communities of the Cistercians and Augustinians sprang up all over Europe in the centuries to follow. Both sought the primitive Gospel, but their emphases were distinct.

The Cistercians considered that the Cluniac reforms were concerned more with splendid ritual and cultured self-sufficiency than with purity of heart, and aimed to restore the original Benedictine Rule. They were concerned, too, about a decline in membership of the Benedictine Orders, which accompanied the drop in endowments from the feudal magnates. They sought 'an exposition of the whole Gospel',[4] which meant, they believed, a withdrawal from society in a new austerity.

While the Augustinians were also impelled by a reaction to abuse and compromise, unlike the Cistercians they sought in various ways to serve society. They honoured the great Augustine, and claimed to be returning, through him, to the Bible. From these two sources they developed a less rigorous Rule, devoting themselves to something of a reconstruction of the fluid society in which they lived. But while the Augustinian Rule was the most popular, the Cistercian movement, with its harsher authoritarianism derived like its members from the military aristocracy, was to prove more in tune with the expansionist spirit of the age.

It was no accident that the chief Crusading Orders adopted the Cistercian Rule. 'The Cistercians,' R.W. Southern writes, 'were essentially a frontier organization engaged in a work of colonization which was partly religious, partly military, and partly agrarian.'[5] So we are back to the strange marriage of asceticism amd military aggression represented by the sword-wielding monks of the Crusades, men who, to their contemporaries, were simply front-line soldiers of Christendom, helping to defend or extend the commonwealth of God on earth.

All attempts to return to the apostolic simplicity of the Gospel, however, overlooked the *sine qua non* of Christianity. Perhaps it was the conversion of John Bernadone, nicknamed Francis, which focused attention on a truth which, by the thirteenth century, the world had almost forgotten, the truth that a man must have an inward and spiritual rebirth.[6] An outward conversion from a secular to a 'religious' life, the renunciation of the world by joining an Order, was not, after all, the unfailing path to God.

4
Poverty, Power, and Protest

Francis, Dominic, and the 'paupers of Christ'
The inspiration provided by St Francis and his early followers, who wished 'naked to follow the naked Christ', was to the heart rather than to the head. St Dominic, originator of the other great Order of friars, the Dominicans or 'Friars Preacher', was responsible for giving the whole movement some coherence. St Francis, whose Rule was approved in 1210 when he and twelve followers placed it before Innocent III in Rome, had little sense of order and tradition. Despite this fact, by 1218, when Francis met Dominic in Rome, there were Franciscans in most of Western Europe.

The Dominican friars followed the rule of St Augustine; the Franciscans were in some senses the heirs of the Cistercian devotion to the person of Jesus. Yet the friars were essentially something new. They belonged to an environment which had scarcely existed a hundred years earlier - that of the great towns and universities. They were religious creations which best met the needs and fitted the social patterns of Western Europe in the thirteenth century.

One element, in particular, was highly favourable to the establishment and growth of friar communities - the emotional intensity of the age. The cycle of plenty, want and communal violence, led to a desire to achieve a new freedom in poverty, with every hope fastened on eternity. Thus groups of flagellants would appear from time to time, parading through the towns barefooted, beating each others backs, wailing and beseeching God's mercy. In these unstable and sometimes even anarchic conditions, so conducive to hysteria, the friars flourished.

Another quite different factor in the success of the friar movement was the intellectual freedom provided by the developing universities - as in Paris and Bologna at the beginning of the thirteenth century. These were strongly patronized by secular rulers, who required scholars as government servants and advisers, a state of affairs that suited the Dominican Order of friars whose aim was to combat heresy through preaching, and which required academic discipline as well as a universal organization.

Dominic, like Francis, wanted a simple 'apostolic' life for his friars, but this was primarily the means to a pedagogical end; the Franciscan movement was one of protest against all worldly glory, wealth, comfort and even organization. The aim was really people's conversion, leading on to a new way of life, that of 'the imitation of Christ'. Francis' challenge was, as we have said, to the heart. The way of life he commended was to be followed by instinct rather than through rules and organization; his was a spiritual revolution.

The Franciscan approach, in particular, touched deep emotional springs within the contemporary urban society. It spoke of destitution - such destitution as prevailed only too commonly - as something to be embraced with joy as the way both of experiencing and commending Christ's salvation. Its universal appeal owed much to the glowing simplicity of its founder; its permanence, in contrast to the transience of movements of a similar nature, like that of the 'Apostles' later in the century[1], probably owed more to the fact that in due course it settled down (somewhat to the dismay of Francis himself) within the framework of an ecclesiastical organization, borrowing much from the Dominicans and following them into the universities.

By the early fourteenth century there were about six hundred Dominican and fourteen hundred Franciscan houses, comprising perhaps twelve thousand Dominicans and twenty-eight thousand Franciscans.[2] The houses, more common in southern Europe than in the north, where the more agrarian Cistercians still predominated, were invariably in the towns; there the friars found the people for whom their message was especially appropriate, there they could win recruits, there they could, as mendicants, find sustenance.

As time went on, however, the friars developed vices related to their lifestyle. They were allowed to possess land and buildings for living and work purposes only, and their poverty made them look for legacies and fees, which in turn encouraged them to treat leniently those amongst their penitents who were also benefactors. They began, in fact, to exemplify some of the very traits against which the movement had initially reacted; the compromise, the worldliness which was all but engulfing the wider Church had crept back into their cells.

Power, corruption, and schism

It was in the thirteenth century, when the friars were flourishing so remarkably, that the Church attained the zenith of her political power; the peak of corruption she scaled in the fourteenth century.

'See, I have this day set thee over the nations and over the kingdoms, to root out, and to pull down, and to destroy, and to throw down; to build and to plant.' So Pope Boniface VIII (1294-1303), in applying the words of Jeremiah to himself, defined the plenitude of Papal power in the Bull *Unam Sanctam*.[3] 'The secular sword is in the power of Peter', he declared.[4] His words sum up the pretensions, and to some extent the actual position, of the Papacy throughout the thirteenth century, a situation further illustrated by the fact that even before the century opened the Popes were claiming the title

'Vicar of Christ', in preference to 'Vicar of Peter', as more perfectly expressing their claim to supreme political, as well as ecclesiastical, authority.[5]

No Pope's power was ever absolute in practical terms, of course, as the career of Innocent III (1198-1216) demonstrates. In 1209, having secured for the Imperial throne the candidate of his choice, and having obtained this Emperor's complete submission to his will, he wrote in his register of letters: 'The state of the world, which is falling into ruins, will be restored by our diligence and care . . . for the pontifical authority and the royal power (both of them supremely invested in Us) fully suffice for this purpose . . .'[6] Within a few months, however, the Emperor, Otto IV, had disregarded his promise, and within two years the Pope was forced to nominate another to the throne - Frederick II, a candidate he had earlier strongly opposed. A ferocious struggle ensued throughout the thirteenth century, with the Papacy seeking control of the Empire; the Emperor was, after all, crowned by the Pope, and should be his principle deputy in the secular sphere, giving crucial support as the Papacy exercised its authority over other rulers.

Even into the fourteenth century and beyond, when it was becoming clear that direct control of secular rulers was doomed to failure, the Papacy used every available means, material as well as 'spiritual', to maintain its secular authority. Yet at the international level its actual power in material terms was insignificant; its main technique, therefore, was to harness 'spiritual' authority to secular ends, promoting alliances, fomenting war, or arbitrating between warring princes, as between England and France in 1345. Papal dispensations were the incentives offered to rulers in all such interventions, with interdicts the main sanction.

Towards the end of the Middle Ages the Papacy tacitly abandoned its claim to universal political supremacy in favour of the role it had been developing as international diplomat and mediator in disputes. Yet in Italy, where the Pope was a secular prince in his own right, John XXIII (the first) was involved in direct warfare with King Ladislas of Naples in 1411, proclaiming the campaign a Crusade, and offering plenary indulgences to those who supported him, and even in the early sixteenth century the Papacy was deploying its own military forces to intervene in the Italian wars. Julius II (1503-13) even revived the Papal claim to universal sovereignty.

In 1309 Pope Clement V moved to Avignon, and there the Papal court remained for nearly seventy years without having any physical contact with Rome. The court's main concern was business, of which three forms of activity predominated; the issue of indulgences, Papal intervention in international affairs, and the appointment of personnel to Papal benefices. It is instructive to trace the development of the first of these business concerns.

The first indulgences to be issued were the plenary indulgences - a full immunity from eternal punishment - which were offered to the Crusaders; then the same immunity was offered by Innocent III to those who helped the

Crusades with money or advice; then a promise of increased rewards in heaven for good works was added to this immunity.[7] By the mid-thirteenth century Innocent IV was granting plenary indulgences in special circumstances without any condition of service at all - first of all to deserving religious individuals, but by the end of the century to secular rulers for political reasons. Soon after this, plenary indulgences were being offered for sale; they were paid for in advance, being granted at the moment of death. In the first six months of 1344 no fewer than two hundred people - knights, parish priests and townsfolk as well as royalty - had been granted this privilege in England alone.[8] Plenary indulgences were next offered to pilgrims to Rome in jubilee years, then, in the later fourteenth century, similar privileges were granted to local churches on special occasions. Finally, the whole system was extended until it covered every conceivable contingency in the life of the sinner, many factors combining to encourage this proliferation: the individual's desire for an assured salvation; the claims of local churches, rulers, and towns to share in the treasure won by the superfluity of Christ's sacrifice; the desire of rival Popes to extend their influence and improve their finances.

And so we come to the fact of Christendom's divisions. For the Church was not only corrupt, it was also doubly divided.

In 1204, when the fourth Crusade, diverted from Jerusalem, had sacked Constantinople, destroying precious manuscripts, rifling churches, and perpetrating many fearful outrages in three days' looting, there had occurred the Eastern Schism - the final severance of the Eastern Church from the Western. In 1378 there occurred the Great Schism, a schism within the Western Church.

There had several times been concurrent Popes before 1378; in that year, however, the separation became definite - Urban VI was elected at Rome, Clement VII at Avignon. Now, therefore, on top of all the manifest abuse and corruption - the system of indulgences, the distortion of the Mass into little more than a vehicle for the acquisition of merit, the neglect of the Bible, the improper veneration of the saints and their 'relics', the lust for and acquisition of worldly wealth, power and glory, the licentiousness, simony, nepotism, absenteeism and pluralism - was the spectacle of two Popes reigning from their thrones, each calling the other Antichrist.

Protest: Wyclif, Hus, and Luther

The start of the Great Schism, and the issue by Pope Gregory XI in 1377 of a series of Bulls condemning his views, radically altered the situation of the Oxford teacher John Wyclif and drove him to the systematic development of his doctrinal and theological ideas that resulted in an unequivocal and detailed condemnation of the Papacy and all it stood for. His was the clearest protest up to that time. Wyclif argued that the only Head of the Church was Christ; there could be no authority or institutionalism within the Church because it was the Body of Christ, composed solely of the 'congregation of the predestined';[9] these were known only to God. The king was God's regent, and had the Christian authority to reform the Church's hierarchy and cut away its corrupting privileges. God's grace was available to every Christian, and the commands of any ecclesiastical leader must be tested by Scripture. Wyclif went on to repudiate not only ecclesiastical authority but also all ecclesiastical privileges or concern for civil affairs, the doctrine of transubstantiation in the Mass, and corrupt and superstitious practices such as pilgrimages, the cult of saints, and the selling of indulgences. In all his arguments he stressed, with growing emphasis, that God's Word, the Bible, was the supreme authority and only justification for any conclusion.

Wyclif died of a stroke in 1384, but his protest was perpetuated in England by his disciples, who became known as the Lollards (an approbrious term for heretics, meaning 'mumblers'), and operated as itinerant lay evangelists. They received only limited popular support, however, and virtually no support from the influential. The movement - unjustly suspected of fomenting revolution - was in fact driven underground through persecution. The translation of the Bible into English was perhaps their greatest achievement.

Wyclif was, however, to influence John Hus, a scholar of Prague University, Bohemia. By the time Hus became Dean of the Faculty of Arts, in 1401, he was already familiar with Wyclif's early philosophical writings; but in 1402 his friend, Jerome of Prague, returned from Oxford with more of Wyclif's work, particularly the *Dialogue* and *Trialogue*, both of which attacked corruption. In 1412, Hus clashed with Pope John XXIII over the sale of indulgences for his Crusade. He condemned the Pope as Antichrist, arguing that only God could absolve from the penalty of sin; he also stated that the Pope should not fight like any secular lord, but deal rather with spiritual matters and use the Word of God.

In 1414 Hus, with a promise of safe conduct from the Emperor Sigismund, attended the General Council of Constance, summoned by John XXIII to end the scandal of three competing Popes, and to stamp out heresy - primarily Wyclifite ideas and the teaching of Hus himself. The promise of safe conduct was abandoned, and after being imprisoned Hus was confronted with forty-five Wyclifite articles and a series of propositions from his own writings, and asked to recant. He refused, was condemned as a heretic and burnt at the stake. Ironically, he was more of a moderate than Wyclif, especially on the question of the Mass. He looked back to his native Bohemian reform movement as well as to Wyclif, and he hoped for a moral change in the existing structure of the Church.

Neither Wyclif nor Hus, despite many of their contemporaries feeling much as they did, was able directly to initiate a wave of protest strong enough to achieve actual reformation - whether within the Church, or by a break-away movement. Yet it was a treatise by Hus on the Church, a work indebted to the teachings of Wyclif, that Martin Luther, the greatest reformer of all, was reading in 1520 a few months before denouncing the Papacy as Antichrist and openly defying all ecclesiastical authority.

Luther had joined the mendicant Order of Augustinian Hermits in 1505, following an intense personal religious struggle during which he made, in prayer to St Anne, a promise to take religious vows. In 1507 he was ordained to the priesthood, and in 1510 he travelled to Rome, where he was shocked by the manifest corruption. Two years later he was awarded a doctorate, which committed him to public speaking and preaching. Yet his spiritual struggle continued. He felt he could not achieve a genuinely pure love of God, nor keep the monastic vows to perfection. Indeed, he later said of his feelings at this time: 'I hated this just God who punished sinners.'[10]

Under the influence of the English Franciscan William of Occam, Luther concluded that he must somehow eradicate every sin and achieve perfect obedience in order to find God's grace. Inevitably he met failure, and a consequent deeper misery. He was advised by the Vicar-General of his Order, John von Staupitz, to do four things: read the German mystics, read St Augustine, think of Christ's wounds and the loving heart of God, and read and reread the Bible.

Luther was not the only monk or friar to search for something deeper within the religious way of life. The German Dominican friar Meister Eckhart had preached in Cologne, at the beginning of the fourteenth century, of an interior conversion of the soul that would manifest itself in the appropriate way determined by God alone, causing all vows, disciplines, and religious exercises to retreat into the background.

Luther's spiritual problem, however, needed an answer more sharply defined than that offered by Eckhart, or any other such mystic. He did not find the solution to his personal need in St Augustine, either, though he learnt from the great theologian that the true Church was invisible - the body of faithful believers. He finally sought to concentrate his mind on the idea of God's love and to turn away from the thought of his judicial righteousness - the divine quality which so terrified him - and this encouraged him to study Paul's Epistle to the Romans with a new care. Though he had been spending much time on New Testament study, using the Greek version of the text edited by Erasmus, he had shunned the Epistle precisely because it referred so frequently to the righteousness of God.

It was in the early spring of 1513, that, turning to Romans 1: 16, 17, Luther found that assurance of forgiveness his heart had so long desired: 'The just shall live by faith.' Of this moment he later wrote: 'It seemed to me as if I were born anew.' And in a commentary on Psalm 31, probably written on the day of this discovery, he wrote: 'Concerning the means of true repentance, that sins are remitted, not by any works, but alone by the mercy of God without any merit.'[11]

Luther's discovery, and the implications of that discovery, were bound in the end to lead him into conflict with the Church authorities, for he was an officially designated preacher - an office that, he was careful to argue, had been pressed and forced upon him. In June 1520, Luther published *The Papacy at Rome*, an exposition of the nature of the Church - possibly influenced, as we have seen, by Hus' treatise *On the Church* which he had recently read. Then, spurred on by his new conviction that the Papacy (but not the individual Pope) was Antichrist, he followed it up with his *Open Letter to the Christian Nobility of the German Nation*. In this tract Luther denied that any visible institution could be identified with the Christian Church, he attacked the political power claimed by the Papacy, and he declared the priesthood of all believers, which meant that the Christian laity could interpret Scripture and call councils. So he called upon the Christian nobility to initiate a movement for ecclesiastical reform, since the clergy 'to whom this task more properly belongs, have grown quite indifferent.'[12] Two more tracts followed closely. In *The Babylonish Captivity of the Church* Luther reduced the sacraments to three, and denied that the Mass was a good work, declaring it to be simply a seal of the Christian's confession of faith. In *Concerning Christian Liberty* he expounded the doctrine of justification by faith.

Luther was at the crossroads. In April 1521 he was summoned before the new young Emperor Charles V, at the Diet of Worms. On being demanded to retract, he made a speech in his own defence, the concluding words of which were these: 'Unless I am proved to be wrong by the testimony of Scriptures and by evident reasoning ... I cannot and will not retract anything, for it is neither safe nor salutary to act against one's conscience. God help me! Amen.'[13]

5
Revolution, Reason, and Revival

The Reformation: a spiritual and political revolution
Luther's protest caused a revolution.

After the Diet of Worms, the sympathetic Elector of Saxony arranged for Luther to be 'kidnapped' on his way home. The 'kidnappers' took Luther to the castle of the Wartburg. He rested there, and for a while felt depressed. Essentially of a conservative temperament, Luther had a dread of social disorder. He had no systematic scheme of authority with which to replace the hierarchy that his own protest was attacking. Having delivered 'the Word', he believed all problems must be solved by that Word[1], and he expressly rejected, at this point, any idea of raising a peasants' revolt. Yet the revolt came.

During the years 1524-5 a series of peasant risings swept through southern Germany. Luther had called for the Christian laity to rise and reform the ecclesiastical potentates, but he believed that this should only be effected through peacable, if insistent, demand. When the angry peasantry burnt convents and castles alike, and initiated a massacre at Weinsberg, Luther wrote a desperate tract, *Against the Murdering, Thieving Hordes of Peasants*, which called upon the princes to 'brandish their swords' and stamp out the revolt.[2] 'I do not wish,' he had written to Ulrich von Hutten in 1520, 'to do battle for the Gospel with force and slaughter. The world is overcome by the Word . . .'[3] He had proved his sincerity in March 1522, when he personally quelled a riot in Wittenberg. But he could not control the peasants; they had heard the call for a Christian country, and, following more radical and apocalyptic preachers than Luther, they responded.

The practical task of forming a Lutheran Church gathered momentum, under the civil authorities. Many princes were sympathetic to Luther's call, and the process began in earnest in 1529 at the second Diet of Speyer, when a 'protest' (the origin of the term 'Protestant') was delivered against the Holy Roman Emperor and the Catholic princes. The protestors became linked in a Protestant league, which in due course concerned itself with political matters, such as the rights of princes against the Emperor. Meanwhile the Catholic princes were unable to take effective action against the Protestants because of threats from the Turks, now in Hungary, along their eastern borders. The Lutheran churches were left to organize themselves.

In 1530 a Lutheran doctrinal statement was presented to the Diet of Augsburg by Philip Melancthon, Luther's partner in reform at this time. Meanwhile, the necessary practical steps were being taken; German Bibles were placed in churches, the liturgy was revised in the German language, rites were supressed and German hymns and catechisms were published, Masses for the dead were abolished, preaching became more common, monks were free to abandon their vows and the civil authority of the bishops was revoked and given to the Electors.

Luther died in 1546, but the revolution lived on. It was a tide already flowing across much of central and northern Europe, whose effects were to be felt far beyond that.

In Zurich, a free Swiss city of the Holy Roman Empire, the process of reform was a relatively tidy affair, having been completed between 1522 and 1525. Bowing to pressure from the leading citizens, who approved the reforming doctrines, the city council legislated reforming measures in the parishes, followed by regulations to control public morals. Zwingli, the main force in this movement, had - to some extent independently - developed ideas similar to those of Luther, through the influence of the Dutchman Erasmus, who, with John Colet and Sir Thomas More, was one of the three Oxford Renaissance reformers.

At Strasbourg the leading light was Martin Bucer, whilst at Geneva it was the Frenchman, William Farel, who was then to hand over the main work of organization to that other great reformer, John Calvin. In 1536 Calvin had published *The Institutes of the Christian Religion* and soon afterwards he was invited to live in Geneva and teach. After being exiled for a period, he was recalled in triumph and thereafter his efficient measures were adopted. His aim was to establish a church in Geneva after the primitive New Testament pattern. Geneva was to become the natural refuge for French Protestants fleeing from persecution, and many of these became the church's pastors.

Calvin's doctrine of God's providence, and its particular application to the idea of predestination, is well known. He took this idea to extremes, teaching that Christ died only for the predestined elect; others, he said, were predestined to damnation. The doctrine was earnestly debated for a century or more, with reformers like Arminius in Holland softening Calvin's teaching by explaining that God's foreknowledge did not eliminate man's free will.

The Calvinists of those times were devout people, fearless and determined in pursuing their mission, and the Swiss pattern of reform became the norm for Protestant churches in Europe outside Lutheran Germany and Scandinavia.

In England the Reformation was more moderate than elsewhere in Europe, differing in the extent to which political factors were involved in the reforming process. 'The Pope would not allow Henry VIII to marry Anne Boleyn when he was already married to Catherine of Aragon, so the king threw off the yoke of the Papacy.' This is the common refrain, which is accurate as far as it goes. Henry's new Archbishop of Canterbury, Thomas Cranmer, declared the marriage with Catherine null and void, and Anne was crowned Queen in 1533. In 1534 the Act of Supremacy declared the king to be Supreme Head of the Church in England. Some objected; Bishop Fisher of Rochester and the ex-Chancellor, Sir Thomas More, were beheaded for refusing to foreswear the Pope's authority. The few open objectors there were, however, were mostly uneducated and lacking influence.

The smaller monasteries were suppressed in 1536, after a visitation during which unsavoury conditions were reported, and in the next few years the larger monasteries 'surrendered' - readily enough, under the persuasion of further visitors. By 1540 the process was complete, the vast majority of abbots accepting the royal supremacy without a murmur. The dissolution of the monasteries was to have far-reaching social consequences. Their influence had extended widely over the surrounding countryside. Conditions within them had not always been shameful, but most houses were highly secularized; few displayed the discipline and devotion of the Carthusians, who accepted death rather than submit to Henry.

It was not until after Henry's death, and the accession of Edward VI in 1547, that doctrinal reform began in earnest. In 1539 Cranmer and Thomas Cromwell had issued the first official English Bible, but in 1549 a new English Prayer Book, modelled on Lutheran principles, was issued. It was followed in 1552 by a version modified in the direction of Zwingli's views about the Mass (now called the Holy Communion). Despite these developments, when Mary succeeded Edward, the general populace of England was only superficially Protestant.

Mary restored the Catholic faith, reaffirming the doctrine of transubstantiation, repealing the Acts against the Pope, and burning unrepentant Protestants. Nearly three hundred of these were burnt at the stake in three and a half years - including the bishops Ferrar, Hooper, Ridley, Latimer and Cranmer.

But Mary died, without issue, in 1558, and with the accession of Elizabeth the way was opened to a permanent settlement. While the Queen favoured a form of Catholicism without the Pope, she came under pressure from the increasing number of convinced English Protestants. In 1559 an Act of Parliament duly decreed that she, as Queen, was Supreme Governor of the Church in England, and the Act of Uniformity substantially restored the Prayer Book of 1552, affirming also that Sunday attendance for every citizen in his parish church was mandatory.

To this day the English monarch has remained Supreme Governor of the Church in England, with the power to appoint bishops and other senior ecclesiastics, although the sovereign's power in this regard was effectively limited at the Restoration of 1660. In modern times the Prime Minister (with

advice from Church leaders) has made the final decisions about appoint-
ments, and Acts of Parliament have been required to effect changes in the
Church's Faith and Order.

It was after 1559 that the English Reformation became a reforming force
in the sense of dispelling superstition and ignorance amongst the clergy and
laity. Meanwhile, in the rest of Europe, the tide of reform continued to flow.
Where the State approved, and took charge, the reforms tended to be
conservative, as in England; where there was government resistance (as in
France and Scotland), it was more radical and Calvinistic, since Calvinism
had organized the ministry as an authority free from state oversight.

The later details of this development should not detain us, apart from a
reference to the Puritans and Anabaptists.

Puritans were strict Christians, usually Calvinistic, who believed that
churches should be organized round the person of the presbyter. They
possessed a strong moral sense, though tended to be intolerant. In worship
they emphasized simplicity, all ornamentation and elaboration being counted
as distraction. Puritanism was an attitude, not a sect, and its adherents were
found in Protestant churches throughout Europe. In England, however, some
extremist Puritans resisted all attempts to include them in the national
Church; these were called the Independents.

Anabaptists, small groups of somewhat diverse doctrine and practice who
met to study the Bible, were found mostly in Switzerland, the Rhineland and
Holland. They usually denied the doctrine of infant baptism, affirming this
view in an Anabaptist Confession of 1527, together with their separation from
the world and anything that smacked of Popery. It was the influence of these
Christians which resulted in the establishment of the first Baptist churches in
London in the early seventeenth century.

Counter-Reformation, war and peace

Protestants were not the only reformers of the sixteenth century; the
movement of reform called the Counter-Reformation, occurring within the
Roman Church, was equally rigorous in its way. Wyclif, Hus, Luther and
other reformers had initially hoped that Rome would be susceptible to
genuinely evangelical reform, and there were others with similar hopes, like
Luther's early friend and mentor, von Staupitz, who never separated themselves from Rome. The success of Luther's own protest, however, and that
of other Protestants, tended to put Rome in a militant mood - towards a fight
against Protestantism - which in turn gave Rome's existing internal drive for
reform a greater impetus. The Inquisition, initially directed against internal
heresy, was a manifestation of this reaction.

A key individual in the Counter-Reformation was St Ignatius of Loyola,
who founded the Order of the Jesuits (the Society of Jesus) in 1540, after a
much earlier spiritual experience analogous in some ways to that of Luther.

Ignatius and his first followers had wished, in 1534, to go to Palestine and work for the conversion of the Turks, but this was impossible and instead they took a vow of absolute obedience to the Pope. This constituted the answer to Ignatius' desire for total commitment. In obedience to this vow, in April 1541, St Francis Xavier, with three other Jesuits, embarked at Lisbon to be missionaries in the Indies, so initiating the Order's remarkable missionary endeavours. The foundation or reconstitution of other Orders in this period - the Capuchins (a return to the primitive Franciscan ideal) in 1528, the Theatines in 1532, the Barnabites in 1533 - was a further manifestation of the reforming spirit within the Roman Church.

A General Council of the Roman Church did not occur until 1545. Its last session was in 1562-3, but when it met it proceeded with a confutation of Protestant doctrines. There were some genuine reforms, however, like the abolition of the office of seller of indulgences, and the establishment of diocesan training schools for candidates for the priesthood.

The Counter-Reformation had its political as well as religious aspect. Indeed, it set in motion a period of religious strife culminating in the Thirty Years War; for, seeing the nature of the Roman reforming zeal, the Protestants of the newly emergent states of Europe became increasingly fearful that the Catholic powers would reimpose Catholicism by force. The fears were fed by the increasing numbers and influence of the Jesuits, whom Protestants suspected, not without reason, of being political agents as well as religious zealots. The strife commenced when France and Spain made peace in 1562, at which point civil war broke out in France. The entire period, which ended in 1629, coincided with a weak and divided France, which allowed the Habsburg powers in Spain, Austria and Italy freedom to operate in concert. This league of Catholic powers was encouraged by Pope Pius V and his successors, and it began to resemble a marshalling of forces for a new military Crusade against Protestantism. Pope Sixtus V arranged wide-ranging alliances, hoping to conquer the Turks, retake Jerusalem and destroy the Protestants. Though the dream was not fulfilled, it had not been altogether unrealistic, for in Germany Protestantism remained divided, and there was some disillusion owing to the failure of the Reformation to achieve its early goals.

In 1608 the Protestant states had formed a defensive Evangelical Union; when, in 1618, the Protestant nobles of Bohemia revolted against Austria, killing the Imperial commissioners and driving out the Jesuits, the Thirty Years War began. It was at first a war of Calvinist against Catholic, but by 1635 it had become a full-scale European war with the antagonists ranged behind France and Germany. The Pope was by now on the sidelines, concerned chiefly with maintaining the Papacy as an Italian princedom. In 1648 the war ended with the Peace of Westphalia, which established the religious boundaries of modern Europe. The Peace constituted a qualified victory for Protestant rulers, and a blow to the Papacy's political aspirations as expressed through the Counter-Reformation.

Whilst the Western Church (and Western Europe) had been set in turmoil by the protest of Luther and other reformers, the Eastern Church was quietly unaffected. After the fall of Constantinople to the Ottoman Turks in 1453, more and more of the Orthodox Church came under Turkish control, and when, in 1589, the Patriarchate of Moscow was created it represented the only Orthodox Church both established and not under Muslim control. Turkish rule over the rest of Orthodoxy, however, had served to ensure that neither the Reformation nor the Counter-Reformation made any impression on Eastern Christendom. In 1559, for instance, the Patriarch of Constantinople, on being shown the Augsburg Confession by a Protestant diplomatic chaplain, replied by suggesting that the Lutherans should accept the teaching of the Orthodox Church.[4]

The two English civil wars, of 1642-5 and 1648, were concerned more with constitutional matters than religion. Yet they indirectly had much to do with the issue of religious freedom.

Certain Englishmen who considered themselves patriots feared that King Charles I and his Archbishop, Laud, would reinstate Roman Catholicism. Laud was executed in 1643 on a charge of treason, including that of trying to reconcile the Church of England with Rome, and after the defeat of the king at Naseby in 1645 Oliver Cromwell and the New Model Army were effectively the rulers of both the country and the Church, though ostensibly they ruled through Parliament. The Commonwealth period proper commenced in 1649, after the king's execution, and lasted until 1660. Under Cromwell the Independents flourished, John Milton, an ardent propagandist for Independency, being one of his secretaries. By 1660 there were about one hundred and thirty Independent ministers in Cromwell's 'established' Church, with other congregations, including Baptists, permitted to worship freely. Only Papists and high Anglicans were excluded from this umbrella of toleration.

Yet because the idea of Anglicanism (the Book of Common Prayer, and the polity of bishops, priests and deacons) became identified with the Royalist position, both Charles I and Laud came to be seen as martyrs to that cause, and at the Restoration of the monarchy the Prayer Book (slightly revised) and the episcopacy were reinstated. Cromwell's religious toleration, however, remained; no machinery of discipline, like the Star Chamber or the High Commission, was revived. The Church of England itself was broad, and nonconformity was acknowledged to be a permanent feature of English life. The achievement was not, of course, wholly that of Cromwell and the other architects of the revolution. The revolt had had its roots in the protest of Wyclif and the Lollards, and in the ferment created in the disciplines of science, history and law by such men as Francis Bacon, Sir Walter Ralegh and Sir Edward Coke.[5]

The Age of Reason, and a religious establishment

Francis Bacon had outlined a new scientific method that was henceforward
to rule the scientific scene; it was his approach to science, and that of
Descartes to philosophy, which inaugurated what has been described as the
'age of reason'.[6]

The new intellectual currents were flowing at a time when Europe,
following the Peace of Westphalia, was exhausted by a century of religious
strife and warfare, with princes and people alike longing for some kind of
stability. The Papacy could no longer manipulate events in Western Europe,
and the Pope could not now claim it as his prerogative 'to destroy, and to throw
down', or to 'build and to plant', either kings or their kingdoms. His greatest
weapon, the Interdict, was no longer feared. In this new age, the Church was
largely to be subordinate to the State; indeed, secular rulers tended to look
upon the Church as their tool in achieving national stability. Their aim was
no longer the establishment of doctrinal truth within the Church; rather was
it the establishment of the Church as a buttress against disorder, and an
upholder of the *status quo*. This, for instance, was the English Prime Minister
Walpole's chief purpose in relation to the English Church of the first half of
the eighteenth century. In other countries rulers would, to serve their ends,
interfere in the Church's affairs, seize her wealth, or alter her structures, and
there was little the national or institutionalized churches could do to oppose
such treatment. Church leaders tended, therefore, to follow the fashion and
devote themselves to theological and philosophical discussion and debate.

To Descartes, who died in 1650, belief in God was central, but such belief,
he taught, should be the product of reason. His views were developed by
others, notably Malebranche and Spinoza, a Jew. Though passionately
upholding the existence of God, Spinoza held that all traditional beliefs
should be abandoned, and his searching examination of man's political
institutions and religious literature persuaded many that Cartesianism was a
dangerous system of philosophy. Blaise Pascal, too, supplied a profound
critique of the Cartesian system.

But the realm of ideas in England at the beginning of the eighteenth
century was dominated by the thought of two men - Isaac Newton, that flower
of the scientific movement under the aegis of the Royal Society, and John
Locke, the Whig philosopher and apologist for the 1688 revolution. The
intellectual achievements of these two men - profound explorations of the
inner natures of the universe and man respectively - were in fact revered on
the continent almost as much as in England. Their achievements paved the
way for the almost universal adoption of the view that unrestricted scientific
research and a latitudinarian and rationalistic approach to philosophy,
political theory, and theology, would find the answer to man's every question
and problem. They also, more practically, encouraged the acceptance of the
principle of religious toleration.

A theological response in England to the new ideas can be seen in the emergence of two groups of thinkers, the Latitudinarians (prominent churchmen, who in due course veered towards Unitarianism) and the Deists. The former sought to reconcile the Church to the new intellectual environment; they taught the benevolent fatherhood of God in an ordered universe, from which flowed man's simple moral duty to show a like benevolence towards his fellows. Speculation about God should cease; man should instead scrutinize himself. A work of John Locke himself, *The Reasonableness of Christianity*, best defines this outlook: Christianity is the religion of reason, and God is the God of Nature. The Deists took the argument further: natural religion was not only a reality (as all conceded), it was sufficient; revelation was at best superfluous, at worst superstitious.

Against these views such thinkers as William Law, George Berkeley and Bishop Butler successfully ranged themselves. Self-confident rationalism received its heaviest blow, however, at the hands of the greatest British philosopher of all, David Hume, whose *Treatise on Human Nature* was published in 1738. Hume exposed the fallacies of an uncritical trust in logic and the human mind. In so doing, however, he demolished all traditional certainties - about God, man and the world. He was vaguely theistic, but the void he left behind him opened the way for a new approach pioneered by Immanuel Kant, whose Deism was grounded in the belief in a moral obligation naturally perceived by man.

Continuous progress in the sphere of scientific investigation - in entomology, mathematics, mechanics and astronomy, for example - tended to encourage religious thinkers to be sceptical as well as rationalistic; Cesare Vanini, a Neapolitan priest who recognized no God but nature, was a notable example. Frontal attacks were made on traditional Christian doctrines, especially in Calvinistic countries like Holland, where the State left the Church to carry on her theological debates unmolested. Richard Simon (1638-1712), a Catholic priest whose primary aim was to confound the Protestants, initiated a critical study of the biblical documents. His views were expanded and popularized with great success in Amsterdam by the Huguenot exile Pierre Bayle, who published a *Dictionary* which became a source book for Deists and sceptics who wished to attack the Bible. The stage was set for the entrance of that most famous Deist - the fiercely anti-clerical rationalist whose thought prepared the way for the French Revolution - Voltaire.

The social scene on the continent during and following the turmoil of the religious wars had been characterized by a breakdown of common morality, especially in Germany. And in England, according to Bishop Secker, 'the distinguishing mark of the present age' was 'an open and professed disregard of religion', reflected in 'dissoluteness and contempt of principle in the higher part of the world' and in 'profligate intemperance and fearlessness of committing crimes in the lower'.[7] The prevailing moral temper of the times has been immortalized for us in the pictures of Hogarth. The scene was fortunately relieved by many examples of personal philanthropy, but it was of a condescending kind - for the poor were all too frequently dismissed as lazy and undeserving.

The established churches had no answer to all this beyond a blanket denunciation of immorality and an exhortation to Godly living. In England, religious fervour, or 'enthusiasm', was condemned by leading divines (especially prelates), theological debate being their main preoccupation besides politics. Preaching from English pulpits (when clerics were in residence, for both pluralism and the involvement in politics led to much absenteeism) was intellectual, with the emphasis on Christianity's ethical demands. Nonconformity in England had also tended to drift into formalism. After the fratricidal fights which immediately followed the Act of Toleration of 1689, the various groups kept a low profile, making little impression on society in general, except through their seminaries, which initiated some significant theological developments. The Independents, known also as Congregationalists, were mostly Calvinistic and concerned with doctrinal purity, the Presbyterians and to some extent the General Baptists moved towards Unitarianism, and the Quakers' energies tended to be expended on their business and banking interests. In Germany, where three main religious bodies were recognized - the Roman Church, the Lutherans and the Reformed (Calvinistic) Church - the position was little different. Intellectualism, strict orthodoxy, and arid theological controversy dominated the two Protestant bodies. Throughout Europe some new and spiritual Christian movement was needed; such a movement was born.

'I felt my heart strangely warmed'

J. Spener, who died in 1705, published a book, *Pia desideria*, which appealed for a revival of the Lutheran principle of personal faith. Through this work, and by his teaching and example, Spener begat Pietism. One of its most notable later figures was Count von Zinzendorf. In 1722 the Count offered a refuge to Moravian Christians fleeing from religious persecution in Habsburg lands, and the community they founded became a centre of evangelical and missionary fervour. Amongst other places to which the Moravian missionaries travelled was the American colony of Georgia, and here, some years later, they were visited by a strict English churchman who had joined the Society for the Propagation of the Gospel (founded by Thomas Bray in 1701 to promote the true religion). In Georgia the Englishman met some of the Moravian brethren, and was profoundly affected by their evangelical piety. Yet, in 1738, he returned to England, feeling that his work overseas had been a failure. Moravians in London kept in touch with him, however, and on Wednesday, 24 May that same year, he very unwillingly attended a Moravian meeting in Aldersgate Street, where one of the assembly was reading Luther's preface to the *Epistle to the Romans*.

This is how John Wesley describes, in his *Journal*, the crucial moment at that meeting: 'About a quarter to nine, while he was describing the change which God works in the heart through faith in Christ, I felt my heart strangely warmed. I felt I did trust in Christ, Christ alone, for salvation; and an assurance was given me that he had taken away *my* sins, even *mine*, and saved me from the law of sin and death.'[8]

One more person had, through the mediation of the Moravians, come to understand the truth that Luther had proclaimed over two hundred years earlier. 'Thus begins', writes G.R. Cragg, 'one of the most remarkable episodes in the history of the church.'[9]

6

The Single Call and a Secular Gospel

A 'remarkable episode' : the evangel for all men

Following his experience in Aldersgate Street, Wesley began to preach the message he had newly understood in whatever churches would open their doors to him - only to find that he was never invited back. But he was not alone. George Whitefield, who had been a friend at Oxford where they had both belonged to the Holy Club, had discovered the way to reach the masses - he preached in the open air. From April, 1739, Wesley began doing the same thing, with extraordinary results.

It has been estimated that Wesley covered a quarter of a million miles during his long ministry, preaching to gatherings which occasionally numbered twenty or even thirty thousand.[1] His friend Whitefield was the more spectacular speaker, with greater power to move the crowds, but Wesley's achievement was in the end the more significant. At first the two of them worked together. Whitefield, however, was a Calvinist, while Wesley followed Arminius in upholding man's freedom of choice. So the two - though remaining friends - began to work separately.

Nor was it in doctrinal matters only that Wesley differed from his friend. He was, unlike Whitefield, very concerned to develop an organization so that his converts would not simply return to their old ways, and it was possibly this concern that accounted for the permanent strength of the Wesleyan revival. He told his converts to form themselves into small groups or 'societies' in order to meet at least weekly for study and mutual exhortation. Members paid a penny each week, which was called 'class money', and adhered to a strict code of conduct in both their private and public lives. By 1746, societies in the same vicinity had been formed into 'circuits' or 'rounds'.

The poor were Wesley's special concern, and he spent most of his time among them, personally raising money to help support the neediest among them. In time, however, the members of his 'Methodist' movement began to prosper, many of them having been turned from wastrals and dissolutes into hard-working, sober and thrifty citizens. Though it may be going too far to suggest that England was saved from a revolution by the preaching of Wesley, it is unquestionably the case that in due course hundreds of thousands of working class people led transformed lives, exemplifying the highest morality, as a result of the achievement of Wesley and, to a lesser extent, that of

Whitefield and other leading figures of the English evangelical revival. The effect of this upon society can easily be underestimated. 'At one point after another', writes G.R. Cragg of the evangelicals, 'their influence stimulated and guided the Christian conscience.'[2] The most famous example of the way the evangelicals helped to change society for the better is probably represented by the campaign to abolish slavery, the success of which was due in no small part to the efforts of the evangelical William Wilberforce.

America also had its revival in this period, usually called the 'Great Awakening'. Jonathan Edwards in Massachussets, Gilbert Tennent in Pennsylvania, a German named Freylinghausen in New Jersey, were preachers who, in the early eighteenth century, were stirring men's hearts and seeing revival fill the churches. But the most influential figure in this New World rebirth of evangelicalism was none other than George Whitefield, who made a number of visits to all the colonies. His preaching had the effect of making coherent what before his contribution had been fragmented.

The Great Awakening had a profound effect on the life of the churches in America, many of them, like the Presbyterians and Baptists, dramatically growing in numbers. Methodism, too, was planted on a wave of enthusiasm, becoming one of the largest churches in North America. The Lutherans and the Reformed Churches were similarly revitalized after having been, up to that time, spiritually comatose. The movement had the effect of enlightening many in America about the evils of slavery, and, under the impetus particularly of the saintly David Brainerd, it opened men's eyes to the Christian duty to evangelize the American Indians.

A fresh awareness of the Christian imperative to evangelize the world was, indeed, perhaps the most notable and permanent result of both the English and American evangelical revivals. In England five major missionary societies were founded under the impulse of the revival. The first was the Baptist Missionary Society, in 1792, after William Carey had written and preached passionately about the obligation upon Christians to work for the conversion of the heathen. Carey was much influenced by the life of David Brainerd as revealed in his diary, and in June 1793, Carey himself left for India as the Society's first missionary. In 1795 the London Missionary Society was founded, followed in 1799 by the Church Missionary Society. The Cornishman, Henry Martyn, whose family had been influenced by the noted evangelical Samuel Walker of Truro, was one of the CMS's earliest missionaries; in 1810 he completed the first translation of the New Testament into Urdu (it remains the basis of the current version), and he then started work on an Arabic translation - all before his death at the age of twenty-nine in 1812. In 1804 the British and Foreign Bible Society was formed, and finally the Methodist Missionary Society was founded in 1813.

The first Protestant missionary to China was Robert Morrison, who arrived from America at Canton in 1807. This was just three years before the foundation of the American Board of Commissioners for Foreign Missions, a mainly Congregational body. In 1814, the American Baptist Missionary Society was formed. The European nations swiftly followed suit, Switzerland leading the way with the formation of the Basel Mission in 1815. Further societies were then formed in Denmark (1821), France (1822), Germany (1824), Sweden (1835) and Norway (1842). Finally, as a result of the Second Evangelical Awakening, which crossed the Atlantic from America to Britain in 1858, the interdenominational missions came into being. The most notable was probably the China Inland Mission, founded by James Hudson Taylor in 1865, which became the largest mission in China.

The Roman Church also saw a revival of missionary endeavour in the nineteenth century - though the impulse to evangelize was rather different from that of the Protestants: the Catholic message told of a salvation which would be achieved through submission to the discipline of the Church rather than through a simple confession of faith. The rise of ultramontanism, emphasising the inherent spiritual authority of the Church as derived from the authority divinely guaranteed to Christ's vicar on earth, the Pope,[3] and the fact that the Catholic Church was no longer under the control of various state authorities, assisted the Papacy in making the Church into a closely-knit body, facilitating its world-wide mission strategy. The doctrine of Papal infallibility, approved almost unanimously on 18 July 1870, by a Vatican Council under Pius IX (the voting taking place during a violent thunderstorm), contributed further to the creation of a unified world-wide missionary offensive, in which the missionaries themselves were untroubled by doubts. The latter were, of course, for the most part members of religious Orders; for during the hundred years following 1815 more new Orders were created than in any previous hundred year period. Most notably, the Jesuits, who had been disbanded in 1773, were reconstituted early in the nineteenth century.

Ecclesiastical retrenchment and theological conflict
Rome's new dogmatism and missionary zeal were perhaps partly a reaction to the waning of the Papacy's temporal power in the nineteenth century. The Pope himself, and most Catholics, had retained the view that the temporal power of the Papacy was essential for the effective exercise of its spiritual power. And indeed, at one stage during this period it almost seemed as if the Pope might become the first President of a democratic federation of Italian states. Such a dream, however, evaporated in 1848, when Rome was overwhelmed by revolutionaries and Pius IX forced to flee. Then, in 1859, most of the Papal states were overrun by the army of Victor Emmanuel II, king of Sardinia, with the support of Napoleon III, and in 1860 Victor Emmanuel was proclaimed king of Italy. In 1870 the Italian armies invaded the Pope's territories, and the kingdom of Italy was formally established. Though free of government control in other countries, in Italy the Catholic Church now

had to acknowledge the State's supremacy; the Papacy's secular power was at an end - apart from the continued existence of a tiny Vatican State.

The Church of England had, of course, been under king and Parliament since the sixteenth century, a state of affairs strengthened by the French Revolution of 1789, which encouraged strong retrenchment within both the ecclesiastical and political forces of conservatism in England. Edmund Burke, in his work *Reflections*, published in 1790, had raised the alarm about the French Revolution. The dangerous doctrinal idealism which inspired it was, he argued, quite foreign to the conservative, pragmatic and gradualist English approach to politics. He pointed to the Church of England as the bulwark of social stability. When Thomas Paine, a confessed republican and unbeliever, published his book *The Rights of Man* in 1791, while the Revolution in France was turning into the bloodshed and chaos of the Terror, leading English churchmen used all their eloquence to denounce revolution in all its forms - ecclesiastical as well as political.

Besides the continuing impact of Pietism, the important Christian developments in Germany in the late eighteenth and early nineteenth centuries were in the realm of philosophical and theological thought. The philosopher Immanuel Kant, who died in 1804, had asked the question: 'What is reason?' He went on to deny the possibility of having a rational theology at all; as regards ultimate reality, the argument from reason could only leave one agnostic. But man's experience of the moral imperative, he added, made belief in God necessary. F.D.E. Schleiermacher (1763-1834) went further, using the fact of man's feeling of absolute dependence as a platform for religious belief - feeling being understood as an intuitive contact with reality. He attached importance to the Church's freedom from state control, teaching that the Church will only be perfected in the final consummation beyond this life. Schleiermacher, who emphasized mankind's solidarity in sin, knew something of the Pietists' evangelical devotion to the person of Christ, and this was reflected in his theology.

During a lifetime which ran almost concurrently with that of Schleiermacher, G.W.F. Hegel poured contempt on his contemporary's views: if a feeling of absolute dependence was the basis for belief, he asked, did it not follow that dogs were the best Christians because they felt such absolute dependence on their masters? He rejected Schleiermacher's teaching that only phenomena can be known by pure reason. Everything, he affirmed, even the Absolute itself, is accessible to the human mind. The world is ordered according to a rational principle, the Absolute Idea, and nature and history are a dialectically evolving process which gradually gives birth to Spirit, a Spirit which has become self-conscious in man. Man at his highest - the philosopher, in fact - can fully apprehend truth as pure thought. For the ordinary person, however, this truth has to be translated into religious pictures and symbols.

The Danish theologian Søren Kierkegaard vigorously attacked Hegelianism and, implicitly, Marxism, with its economic determinism based on Hegel's thought. Kierkegaard protested against the collectivism of the rationalists, and their depersonalization of the individual. God was the Wholly Other, whom the individual must meet in personal experience. The advances in the natural sciences he viewed with suspicion, considering 'sciencemongery' especially dangerous when it invaded the realm of the spirit. As for the Church, it was apostate; indeed, a State Church simply could not be a true church. New Testament Christianity was, in fact, no longer to be found on the earth. But Kierkegaard's challenge, which reached its climax shortly before his early death in 1855, fell on deaf ears; some church people in Denmark said he had gone mad.

Parallel developments; biblical criticism, Christian Socialism, and a new scientific theory

It was the German thinkers, especially Hegel, who most influenced the thought of the English philosopher, theologian and poet, Samuel Taylor Coleridge (1772-1834). Coleridge was an inquirer, and his views were seldom fully worked out. He was particularly impressed by German studies in biblical criticism, and he was one of the first in England openly to question the accepted idea of the plenary inspiration of the Bible and the notion that the truth of Christianity could be established by reference to the fulfilment of biblical predictions or to miracles. The divinity of Scripture, he argued, lay in its power to evoke personal faith in the reader. Another writer whose thought he drew upon was the founder of British Socialism, Robert Owen. Owen, a factory owner who demonstrated that workers' conditions could be improved without loss of profit, was an anti-clerical and utopian agnostic; Coleridge, however, was strongly attracted to his philosophical idealism. Coleridge's teaching on the other-worldly nature of the true Christian Church, whose only head is Christ, was an important and useful emphasis, but his view that the Church should be the nucleus, instructor and a financial executor of the 'Clerisy' (roughly, the nation's benevolent Establishment), was far from orthodox.

Frederick Denison Maurice, who lived from 1805-72, a generation later than Coleridge, made no secret of his debt to the latter. The two of them exerted a tremendous influence on future theologians, and therefore on the future course of Protestant Christianity. Like Coleridge, Maurice took a broad view of truth, both theological and philosophical, and was impatient with those who condemned the new critical approach to the Bible.

Maurice was the son of a Unitarian minister. He joined the Church of England, read theology at Oxford, and was ordained. In the early 1830s he seemed to be an ally of the Tractarians - the High Church leaders of the Oxford Movement, J.H. Newman, J. Keble, E.P. Pusey and H. Froude - who wished to reaffirm the Church of England's heritage as a true branch of the one Catholic and Apostolic Church. These men, who led the Oxford Movement during its most active period from 1833 to 1845 (when Newman seceded to Rome), wrote a series of ninety tracts in defence of the Church's rites and institutions. In due course, however, Maurice took exception to a tract published by Pusey on baptism; it expressed a view about humanity which was incompatible with Maurice's own universalism - for Maurice held that all men by birth reside under the headship of Christ, and that they are not, as Pusey argued, in the grip of Satan until rescued through baptism. 'The truth is,' he wrote, 'that every man is in Christ; the condemnation of every man is that he will not own the truth; he will not act as if this were true.'[4] For Maurice the Church represented the universal family, a redeemed humanity. The philosophy of the French philosophers Bayle, Montesquieu, Voltaire and Diderot (who had all built upon basic concepts from Locke and Newton) had, he believed, rediscovered this truth, and the French Revolution of 1789 had blazoned it - a new humanitarianism - before the world. In the Catholic revival of the eighteen-thirties in France and Britain he discerned a similar awareness of a universal society.[5]

One of Maurice's close friends was John Malcolm Ludlow (1821-1911). He helped Maurice with the production of his publications, and introduced him to the Chartists and the Co-operative movement. The two of them, with Charles Kingsley and a number of other churchmen, were the founders of what came to be called the Christian Socialist movement. Ludlow, a layman who had been educated in France and subsequently met some of the French socialists and social Catholics, supported the French revolution of 1848. In that year he wrote to Maurice that 'Socialism . . . must be Christianized'.[6] The two of them, together with Kingsley, issued a series of tracts entitled *Politics for the People*. Kingsley was the best equipped to write persuasively for the common man, but Maurice provided the theological base for the movement's attack on *laissez faire* and the competitive spirit, as well as for its assertion that men should co-operate and so realize their true nature as children of God and brothers in Christ.

Following the publication of these tracts, the Christian Socialist leaders held discussions with the Chartists, and then initiated the formation of co-operative associations. In time Maurice realized that working men were not sufficiently educated to manage their own affairs, so he set up the Working Man's College, of which he became the first Principal.

The Christian Socialist movement ceased to exist as a formal organization in 1854, but in 1877 the Guild of St Matthew - a fusion of Tractarian and Christian Socialist ideals - was founded by S.D. Headlam (1847-1924). It was a ginger group that adopted shock tactics in order to arouse the conscience of Christians and to press for government legislation to alleviate social injustice. Then, in 1889, the Christian Social Union was founded. Its character and aims were similar to those of the Guild of St Matthew, but it was larger, more respectable and more academic. It also drew on other intellectual sources, such as the idealist philosophy of T.H. Green (1836-82), whose unconventional religious views were typical of Victorian intellectuals - views that, combined with the new uncertainty about Scripture (especially following publication of the symposium *Essays and Reviews* in 1860), encouraged a rethinking of the Gospel.[7] The Christian Social Union began less flamboyantly than the Guild of St Matthew, concentrating its efforts on disseminating the idea that the Christian faith was concerned with the whole ordering of the life of man in society. Its first President was Brooke Foss Westcott.

While socialist-collectivist idealism and biblical criticism were constituting a double assault upon evangelical (and Catholic) orthodoxy, the development of the natural sciences represented an assault from a third direction.

'Theologians and historians - even human intelligence itself - has capitulated to science,' writes the church historian, Philip Sherrard. 'To understand the truth of this statement one has only to take into account the degree to which theologians accept the hypothesis of evolution . . . as axiomatic, and treat it as a kind of imperative condition to which everything, including theology itself, must accommodate itself.'[8] In 1844 Robert Chambers published (anonymously) *The Vestiges of the Natural History of Creation*. In this book he introduced the public to the idea (not in itself new) that a uniform natural law governed the appearance of the various species. It was fifteen years later, however, when Charles Darwin published *The Origin of Species*, that the furore occurred, for he appeared to substantiate the theory of evolution with the data he presented. Though there were contemporary scientists, like Sir Richard Owen, who remained unconvinced, and though there were strong initial protests from leading churchmen, it was not long before Tractarian theologians like F.J.A. Hort and Aubrey Moore, and leaders of the Christian Socialist movement like Stewart Headlam, were accepting and openly proclaiming the Darwinian hypothesis as - in effect - part of God's continuing revelation of the truth to his people. Moore (1848-90) wrote that 'apart from the scientific evidence in favour of evolution, *as a theory* it is infinitely more Christian than the theory of "special creation" . . . Order, development, and law are the analogue of the Christian view of God.'[9] The idea of a gradual evolution of all life under uniform laws, and the concomitant idea of human progress, moral as well as biological, were baptized into Christianity. Such views were, of course, beautifully congruous with the idealist presuppositions of Christian Socialism.

The whole intellectual climate of the time - scientific, philosophical, political, theological - seemed perfect for the swift and successful dissemination of the Christian Socialist viewpoint. The movement possessed a great asset, too, in the Socialist Union's first President, the scholarly and admired

B.F. Westcott. In 1887 Westcott was writing about the social lessons to be deduced from the person of Christ. 'If the Word became flesh, the brotherhood of men is a reality for us,' he declared.[10] 'The brotherhood of men seen in Christ . . .' he explained further 'rests upon the present and abiding fatherhood of God . . . We may acknowledge this God-made kinmanship, or we may neglect it; but none the less we all are . . . brethren in Christ, brethren for evermore.'[11] This fact, together with other doctrinal extrapolations from Christ's person, 'must be taken as the basis of our social scheme.'[12] From this premise he argued that to 'lay the foundations of a social brotherhood . . . is a work of the Church now.'[13] Or again, that 'on the Church then generally lies the responsibility of bringing home to men the thought of international concord, of international co-operation.'[14] The 'concord' and 'co-operation', he wrote elsewhere, follows from 'the solidarity of mankind'; it is 'the natural expression of a unity'.[15] Westcott saw socialism as the antithesis of individualism, which he condemned: 'Individualism and Socialism correspond with opposite views of humanity . . . Socialism is fulfilment of service: the aim of Individualism is the attainment of some personal advantage, riches or place of favour.'[16]

Westcott's universalism, which he shared with Maurice - his assertion, oft repeated, that 'all men are brethren in Christ',[17] *whether or not they respond to him* - was, of course, a very significant shift away from the evangelical doctrine of justification, and adoption into the family of God, by faith through grace. It is the idea which, more than any other, underpins the whole structure of Christian Socialism.

Westcott was, of course, an Anglican bishop, but his teaching that 'we are called . . . to proclaim a gospel to society and not only to individuals'[18] was being echoed by voices within Methodism. The Welshman, Hugh Price Hughes (1847-1902), editor of *The Methodist Times*, persuaded Methodists that the Christian message was a social gospel - that the Gospel delivered to the first Christians by Christ should be interpreted in political as well as spiritual terms. Hughes was also active in encouraging nonconformist unity, and in part it was his efforts that, in 1892, brought about the first Free Church Congress. It is a measure of how far Christian Socialist views had spread into the nonconformist churches that a prominent Congregationalist, R.W. Dale, absented himself from that meeting precisely because he feared that nonconformists were going to organize themselves for political purposes instead of restricting their aim - as evangelicals had traditionally affirmed they should - to that of making individual Christians who would then be socially and politically responsible. In America, too, Protestant theologians were now espousing a social gospel by talking about building the Kingdom of God on earth.[19] This development was strengthened by a reaction to 'fundamentalism' - the name given to the theological views declared by conservative evangelicals at a Bible Congress at Niagara in 1895.

The twentieth century: Christian Socialism and the ecumenical movement
The end of the nineteenth century saw a growing trend within Protestantism
towards the co-operation of the different church denominations, and this, in
part, can be seen as a response to the desire amongst many Christians to work
together in applying the Gospel in the socio-political sphere. The ecumenical
movement, as these efforts towards unity amongst Christians (apart from the
Catholics) came to be called, inspired a number of world conferences; indeed,
the movement burgeoned and flourished, becoming perhaps the most prominent aspect of the Christian scene. The Universal Christian Congress on Life
and Work held at Stockholm in 1925, and which declared for a 'Christian
internationalism', was in some senses an expression of the prevailing
Christian Socialist theology.[20] William Temple was deeply involved in it,
having presided over a conference held in Birmingham by the British
churches the previous year, where the themes were 'Politics, Economics, and
Citizenship'. The desire for a unified effort in world mission was, of course,
another impulse behind the ecumenical movement, the International Missionary Conference of 1910 in Edinburgh usually being seen as the moment
of its birth. A third strand in the movement was described as 'Faith and Order',
for which the first world conference was held at Lausanne in 1927. One of the
two Church of England delegates to this was Bishop Charles Gore, who
succeeded B.F. Westcott as the chief Anglican spokesman for Christian
Socialism.

The 'Life and Work' and 'Faith and Order' strands within the ecumenical
movement were fused when the World Council of Churches (W.C.C.) was
inaugurated at Amsterdam in 1948. Roman Catholics, a few conservative
Protestant groups, and the Russian Orthodox Church declined to attend - the
latter condemning the W.C.C. as a non-ecclesiastical body with political
aims. The Second Assembly of the W.C.C. was held at Evanston, U.S.A. in
1954, when the theme was 'Christian Hope', and a strong statement was
adopted on the race relations issue - an issue that tended to dominate the
business of future assemblies. In 1960 a delegation of the W.C.C. met leaders
of the member churches in South Africa to discuss the inter-racial situation,
and the same year saw the creation of a W.C.C. Secretariat on Racial and
Ethnic Relations. In 1966 the World Conference on Church and Society in
Geneva was discussing 'Theology and Revolution', and in 1968 the Fourth
Assembly of the W.C.C. at Uppsala, Sweden, called for a crash programme
on racism. 1969 saw the Programme to Combat Racism launched, with a
Special Fund to assist the racially oppressed.

By November, 1975, when the W.C.C.'s Fifth Assembly was held in
Nairobi, with the theme 'Jesus Christ Frees and Unites', a sum of somewhere
near half a million pounds had been allocated to numerous 'liberation
movements' round the world, some of them espousing terrorism. The
Anglican churches in South Africa and Rhodesia had opposed such grants,

the former querying, in 1973, the honesty of the W.C.C.'s assertion that such grants were only for humanitarian purposes. Greek and Russian Orthodox leaders were also, in 1973, severely critical of the W.C.C.'s stance.[21] These protests followed a W.C.C. Conference held in Bangkok in early 1973, with the theme 'Salvation Today', and a subsequent meeting of the Commission on World Mission and Evangelism, where pleas were made for further help for movements of political liberation. In 1974 and 1975 there was continuing criticism of the W.C.C.'s support for liberation movements, as well as for its proposal for a moratorium on evangelism.[22] Christian Socialism had now come into full flower.

A century of Anglicanism

Westcott, Gore and Temple were bishops of the Church of England. It is instructive to see how their Christian Socialist ideas prevailed within the Anglican Church. The Lambeth Conferences of bishops, and other similar Anglican conferences, provide a good framework for this.

The Lambeth Conference of 1888 considered how far socialism and Christianity were compatible; it decided that they were not contradictory. In 1897 the Conference was considering 'International Arbitration' and 'Industrial Problems'. Bishop Westcott subsequently commented that these two subjects 'were submitted to the Bishops because it was assumed that they would consider them in the light of the central truth of the Incarnation'.[23] The Conference of 1908 considered a report entitled: 'The moral witness of the Church in relation to the democratic ideal and economic planning'; at a Pan-Anglican Conference in the same year Bishop Gore, then Bishop of Birmingham, pronounced: 'We must identify ourselves with the great impeachment of our present industrial system. We must refuse to acquiesce in it. But more than this, we must identify ourselves, because we are Christians, with the positive ethical ideal of socialist thought.'[24] In 1920 the Lambeth Conference called on 'all Christian people' to accept 'as the basis of industrial relations the principle of co-operation'. Church members, it affirmed, must recognize 'the necessity of nothing less than a fundamental change in the spirit and working of our economic life.'[25]

A conference, similar to the one held at Birmingham in 1924, took place at Malvern in 1941, and once more, William Temple, now Archbishop of Canterbury, presided. As chairman he was personally responsible for the drafting of the resolutions. Amongst other things, the Conference called for public ownership of 'the principal industrial resources', arguing that 'a way of life founded on the supremacy of the economic motive . . . is contrary to God's plan for mankind', and announced that 'the existing industrial order . . . tends to recklessness and sacrilege in the treatment of natural resources . . . has led to the impoverishment of the agricultural community . . . and is largely responsible for the problem of "mass man" . . .'[26] The ideas discussed at this Conference were reflected in Temple's *Christianity and Social Order*, published the following year (and republished in 1976), a book that has had a continuing impact. The drift of the argument it enshrines may be gauged from a single assertion in it: 'No one doubts that in the post-war world our economic life must be "planned" in a way and to an extent that Mr Gladstone (for example) would have regarded, and condemned, as socialistic.'[27] In the year of this book's publication the British Council of Churches was constituted under Temples's leadership, and this body further reflected his Christian Socialist stance.[28] The fundamental premise of that stance - a premise identical to that of his predecessor, B.F. Westcott, whom he greatly admired - can be seen in another of Temple's books, *Hope for the New World*: 'God . . . is the Father of all men' and 'each man . . . is a child of God.'[29]

Although Christian Socialism has been a prevailing viewpoint amongst Anglican church leaders since the time of Temple, with Lambeth Conferences from 1968 implying that even armed revolution could be on the Christian agenda, the picture has not at any time been completely monochrome. Hensley Henson, Bishop of Durham and a contemporary of William Temple, unambiguously expressed the older, evangelical view: 'It is fundamental in Christ's religion that the redemption of the world must be effected through the redemption of individuals. Christian history is filled with failures of attempts to reverse the order.'[30] Few other voices of influence in the ecclesiastical sphere have joined Henson, however. Bishops like Trevor Huddleston, in the Catholic tradition,[31] and David Sheppard, in the evangelical tradition,[32] have ensured that both wings of the Church of England retain Christian Socialist presuppositions. The corporate involvement of the Church in the socio-political sphere is now an assumption that is rarely disputed at any level. For those, like Edward Norman, or other less influential Christians, who seek to restate the old evangelical orthodoxy on this point, 'refutations' are usually published swiftly and have the blessing of ecclesiastical heavyweights; indeed, Anglicans of the 1990s have an Archbishop of Canterbury who has expressly given notice that he will be presiding over a politically active church.[33]

The Church 'politicized'; a form of apostasy

So, in these latter days we have what Edward Norman has described as a 'politicized' Church.[34] As the reader will be well aware, it is now the norm for Councils of Churches, Missionary Societies, Lambeth Conferences, leading Free Churchmen, Catholic Encyclicals, and even local churches of various denominations, to make political pronouncements, or call for an increased political involvement by the Church.[35] Sometimes the call is for the Church to support (or at least to countenance) violence not dissimilar to that perpetrated by the first century Jewish Zealots.[36] The whole movement of 'liberation theology', so widely affirmed today, assumes just such a stance.[37]

Norman's definition is therefore appropriate; the point need not be laboured.

Christians who preach a political gospel would not necessarily, of course, deny that the Gospel also has a spiritual dimension; most argue that a fulfilling of the Church's spiritual role and her alleged political role must somehow be combined.[38] Yet we have seen what the adoption of a political role for the Church can lead to in the call for a moratorium on evangelism proposed by the Bangkok Conference of the World Council of Churches. Christian Socialism always tends to the neglect, or inefficacy, of the Church's spiritual work since time and energy are dissipated on the endless demands of the 'political role', the fulfilment of which often involves the moral condemnation, and consequent alienation, of a section of the public to which the spiritual message of forgiveness and new life is supposed to be on offer.[39] Sometimes, however, as at Bangkok, the spiritual role of the Church is actually denied. In the latter case, apostasy is complete - for apostasy is the identification of the Kingdom of Heaven with the kingdoms of this world.

The temptation to make precisely such an identification was resolutely resisted by the Founder of the Church throughout his ministry until his death in AD 30.[40]

Part II
The Seed

7
The Jesus of History

The sources

What do we make of this man Jesus, who stepped quietly on to the stage of history, whose adult life was so short, but who caused so profound a revolution?

First of all, can we be certain that he really existed?

The answer can only be affirmative. Those who wish to dispute the claims of Christianity never seem to use the argument that the story about Jesus in the New Testament is simply fiction. The question 'Did a man called Jesus of Nazareth really exist?' is posed in Joachim Kahl's savage indictment of the Christian faith, *The Misery of Christianity*. But the verdict is unequivocal: 'Which hypothesis does greater justice to the available source material,' writes Kahl, 'the assumption that a historical figure was deified and raised to the level of a celestial being by his followers ... or the opposite assumption that what was in the first place a myth was subsequently made into a historical figure? ... The second view ... gives rise to more problems than it solves and cannot be made to harmonize with the guaranteed results of form-criticism ... I shall - together with the overwhelming majority of biblical scholars - assume, in the paragraphs that follow, that the Jew, Jesus of Nazareth, did in fact exist as a historical figure.'[1]

Kahl goes on to argue that little can be known about the life and teaching of that historical figure,[2] but his arguments fail to convince. This is mainly because they are based on an inappropriate deduction from a fact about historical research. Kahl rightly points out that 'all historical knowledge, including that of Jesus, has the value of pure probability, never of certainty'.[3] From this truth, however, Kahl appears to argue that we can dismiss as irrelevant, for all practical purposes, findings from research into Christian origins because in the end we have to dismiss as irrelevant all findings of historical research. This is a *reductio ad absurdum*. Nearly all the 'convictions' we hold, and therefore the 'rational' actions we take, spring from incomplete data. Our decisions have to be made on the basis of a balance of probability. Seldom - if ever - are we absolutely sure about anything.

Kahl is also guilty of sweeping assertions about what in fact research into Christian origins has revealed, or can reveal. For example, he baldly declares that 'critical research into the gospels has ... proved conclusively that all the stories of miracles . . . are in fact myths or legends'.[4] Or again, he states that 'it is impossible to reconstruct the preaching of Jesus'.[5]

In relation to the historical reasons which led to the crucifixion of Jesus, Kahl mentions three possible solutions to the problem: that Jesus' death was the necessary conclusion to his preaching, which was so opposed to traditional Judaism that the Jewish religious leaders had to get rid of him; that Jesus was executed by the Romans as a messianic prophet because they did not recognize the unpolitical character of his role; that Jesus was a political revolutionary. He concludes: 'Can anyone decide between these three possible explanations? . . . we may as well freely admit that we just do not know.'[6] From this conclusion Kahl asserts that 'the name of Jesus is empty'.[7]

Kahl's assumptions about our inability to know anything conclusive about Jesus do not simply conflict with the views of Christian theologians;[8] they conflict with the views of most other people who attempt to dispute the claims of Christianity. The Jewish writer Hugh Schonfield, for instance, believes that there is a sufficient platform of fact in the records we have to warrant his own conclusions about Jesus and early Christianity. These are, firstly, that Jesus mistakenly believed himself to be the Messiah of Israel foretold by the prophets, and deliberately plotted his actions in the last fateful week of his life to bear out the messianic prophecies, and, secondly, that after Jesus' death the 'Nazareans' (the primitive Jewish Christians) formed an anti-Roman messianic movement which took up the Zealot cause, though in a non-combatant role.[9] Another writer who examines Christian origins but rejects the claims of Christianity, Rupert Furneaux also assumes such a platform of fact because he uses the gospel accounts freely in his reconstruction of events, though he also claims that 'the Gospel and Acts reflect the beliefs of second-generation Christians *at the time when they were written*, half a century *after* the crucifixion'.[10]

It is not the primary concern of this book to argue the truth of the traditional claim that Jesus was divine, and that his divinity was attested by his corporeal rising from the dead. Others have argued this effectively.[11] Our concern is to examine, on the assumption made by such writers as Schonfield and Furneaux that the New Testament documents are substantially reliable, what Jesus believed to be his role, what he taught his followers to go and do in his name, and why he died. There is, of course, a measure of truth in the words of Furneaux quoted above. Jesus wrote nothing himself; for the views that Jesus held about himself we are therefore necessarily dependent upon the record of his life and teaching made by early Christians. In this sense it is true to say that the New Testament documents give us the picture held of him by the primitive Church, not in a direct sense a picture he himself provided for us.

Yet even if we conceded that all the gospels as well as Acts had emanated from *second*-generation Christians, as Furneaux declares, two important facts would have to be borne in mind. Firstly, thirty or forty years - even half a century - is not a long time where the question is a matter of historical verification. What your parent, or your friend, tells you he has seen or heard or done is not likely to suffer much distortion in that single telling. When a modern biographer uses the memories of those who knew his subject personally, critics do not usually protest that the writer is basing his account on sources that are of questionable veracity; on the contrary, most people would consider such source material to be intrinsically authoritative. Secondly, it is a fact that - unless we give up any attempt (like Kahl) to reconstruct something of the life and teaching of Jesus - we are all of us forced to find data for our reconstruction in the gospels and other documents of the New Testament. For better or for worse, everyone's judgement about Jesus has to be formed on the basis of what his followers recorded. If internal evidence really forces us to discount their testimony as hopelessly garbled and unreliable, so be it. But to dismiss what these people say just because they were 'partisan' is like dismissing what a son says of his father, or what anyone says about someone he admires.

In fact, of course, there are reasons for believing that the gospels, as well as the rest of the New Testament, were written by or had the authority behind them of *first*-generation Christians.[12] If this is indeed so, it must be true that we have a larger number of contemporary sources about Jesus than about any other figure in ancient history.

What, then, can we conclude about the man Jesus - his teaching, his claims, his life and death?

A Spiritual Kingdom

At the very outset of Jesus' ministry, according to three of the four gospel accounts, we have recorded a crucial experience that he endured; it is a period of severe temptation, when he rejected three options that lay before him.[13] The manner of this temptation has no doubt been described for us in symbolic rather than literal terms; they may indeed stand for mental battles that Jesus endured throughout his ministry. But however we view the way in which these temptations actually afflicted Jesus, we can only conclude (assuming we do not, with little reason, dismiss them as fabrications of the evangelists) that the account of them came from Jesus himself. Indeed, the highly pictorial language is exactly what we would expect from the lips of one who was a master story-teller.[14]

What are these options that Jesus rejected?

First of all, Jesus refused to use his special powers to make stones into bread. We are told that during that special time of testing in the wilderness Jesus became hungry as a result of fasting. At one level, therefore, his refusal to 'command that these stones be made bread' was simply a refusal to pander to his own hunger. Yet the reason he gave for refusing - cast in the form of words addressed to the devil - suggest something deeper: 'It is written,' Jesus is recorded to have said, 'Man shall not live by bread alone, but by every word that proceeds from the mouth of God.'[15] He is saying, in fact, that there is something far more important in life than the satisfaction of bodily needs, the provision of bodily sustenance. What is really important is the provision of spiritual sustenance. Here, surely, there is a clear indication that Jesus, at the outset of his ministry, was rejecting an interpretation of his mission that would mean devoting himself to the work of providing for man's physical needs.

Jesus' second temptation, in the order given us by Matthew (who appears to be intending to give us - unlike Luke - a chronological, or logical, order), was that of challenging God to support and preserve him whatever he chose to do - like throwing himself off a pinnacle of the Temple. In so doing he would be forcing God to confirm his unique status. He rejected the temptation with the words 'You shall not tempt the Lord your God'.[16] This was perhaps not only the rejection of the temptation to prove his identity to himself, but also the rejection of a temptation to prove his messianic identity before the world by performing some extraordinary feat - again a refusal to follow the way of the world, the way of worldly success, the way to win worldly acclaim.

The third temptation is perhaps the most significant. Jesus is shown all the kingdoms of the world and their glory.[17] These kingdoms were, the account informs us, in the power of Satan, for Satan himself was going to hand them over to Jesus if he would submit. What does this temptation envisage? C.H. Dodd puts it succinctly: 'He might gain power by "doing homage to the devil" ... or, in realistic terms, exploiting the latent forces of violence to wrest from Rome the liberation of his people.'[18] As with the other two temptations, Jesus expressly rejects such an idea - though, as Dodd points out, 'later . . . there was a moment when he might have been tempted to do so.'[19] 'You shall worship the Lord your God', Jesus replies to the devil's cajolery, 'and him only shall you serve.'[20]

From the very beginning of his ministry, therefore, the Jesus we are presented with by the evangelists is a figure who uncompromisingly eschewed the role of social reformer, public hero or political revolutionary. At various later points in his ministry, and especially during the last climactic week in Jerusalem, Jesus maintained that stance. According to the records, he spent much time in teaching, he twice fed a multitude, he healed the sick, he declared the forgiveness of men's sins, he cast out demons, he raised the dead.[21] Whatever exactly we make of these activities, what is significant is the fact that he was highly selective about them all; only a few of the vast numbers of the world's needy were blessed by him in these ways. And although these activities were not in any way divorced from his spontaneous feeling of compassion for people, it is made clear in the gospels that they were, when meeting people's physical needs, conceived as *signs* of some deeper, and spiritual concern - signs addressed, moreover, to those who were already in some measure responding to him, not to those who were unbelieving.[22]

There was no question of forcing belief on anyone; to have done so would have been to succumb to the second temptation.

One incident in Jesus' ministry is of the greatest significance for us.

John's gospel, like the other three gospels, records for us the feeding by Jesus of some five thousand people from the meagre resources of five loaves and two fish.[23] But John, unlike the other evangelists, records an incident which followed immediately after that remarkable event. The crowds, John tells us, had realized that something quite abnormal had occurred, so that they exclaimed: 'This is indeed the prophet who is to come into the world!' Then John continues: 'Perceiving then that they were about to come and take him by force to make him king, Jesus withdrew again to the mountain by himself.'[24]

C.H. Dodd's analysis of this incident, reported in a single verse, is worth quoting in full: 'In that brief phrase John passes over what must have been a gravely critical situation. It was no less than an attempted rising against the government with Jesus as leader. If he had been a "Messiah" of the common sort it was a golden opportunity; but that sort of messiahship he had long ago rejected as a temptation of the devil. It remained to put an end to a situation which threatened to compromise his whole mission. First, the disciples must be isolated from dangerous contacts. He "compelled" them, Mark says (as if they were reluctant to leave the exciting scene),[25] to take to the boat and cross the lake - and that at nightfall and with a storm brewing. Then he used his remaining influence with the crowd to induce them to disperse peacably, and retired in solitude to the hills.

'So read, the narrative fits aptly into its place in the turbulent history of first-century Palestine. As the church moved outwards and made its appeal to wide circles in the Graeco-Roman world, who could not have cared less about the internal tensions of that distracted country, the political side of the story lost interest. It was forgotten except in one branch of the tradition, that followed by John.'[26]

So, when confronted with the real possibility of casting himself in the role of a political leader, Jesus spurned the idea. But his action only illustrated what he consistently taught about himself and his kingdom, as a few of the sayings ascribed to him will illustrate.

On one occasion the Pharisees - the most zealous and orthodox of the Jewish religious parties - put a question to him. Once again, the incident as reported is very brief, but what Jesus said by way of reply is seminal to his teaching. 'Being asked by the Pharisees when the kingdom of God was coming, he answered them, "The kingdom of God is not coming with signs to be observed; nor will they say 'Lo, here it is!' or 'There!' for behold, the kingdom of God is within you." '[27]

The kingdom which Jesus was calling upon men to enter was therefore not to be an outward or political kingdom.[28] It was a kingdom which was to exist

solely in the hearts of its members. It was, in other words, to be a spiritual
kingdom. Jesus teaching in general underlines this simple truth. The kingdom's ethics, for instance, outlined in the 'sermon on the mount',[29] are
concerned less with the outward act of sin than with the inner and sinful
motive; the parables of the kingdom[30] stress the fact that the kingdom is
something personal, private - almost secret: it is 'seed' which can be 'sown',
as a word or idea is sown, it is like a field in which both 'good seed' and
'weeds' have been sown, it is a 'grain of mustard seed', it is 'like leaven', it
is 'like treasure hidden in a field', it is 'like a merchant in search of fine pearls'.
Finally, it is 'like a net'; this parable, and the parable of the 'good seed' and
the 'weeds', point to a future aspect of the kingdom, that of judgement. But
the judgement is to be effected not by men, but by the 'Son of man' and 'his
angels'.[31]

     Jesus' teaching about life's meaning continues the theme - that outward
and material welfare and success are, though not inherently bad, to be counted
as secondary, and of no ultimate significance. So he counsels his followers
not to 'fear those who kill the body, but cannot kill the soul';[32] he tells them
that 'he who finds his life will lose it, and he who loses his life will find it',[33]
or that 'unless a grain of wheat falls into the earth and dies, it remains alone;
but if it dies, it bears much fruit', so that 'he who loves his life loses it, and
he who hates his life in this world will keep it for eternal life'.[34] He takes a
little child and says that 'whoever humbles himself like this child, he is the
greatest in the kingdom of heaven'.[35] All the normal values of our material
world Jesus reverses; poverty may be more blessed than wealth, failure than
success, death than life. Why? Because his kingdom is spiritual, not material.

Why Jesus lived; why he died

Jesus' teaching about himself emphasizes the same spiritual ideas, and, in
particular, his teaching and actions during the last week of his life seal what
he had said and done up to that time. What then did Jesus say about himself
and his role according to the accounts we have?

     Jesus claimed to have God as his Father; he claimed to be lord of the
sabbath; he claimed to have the power to control nature; he claimed to have
the authority to forgive sins; he claimed the right to judge and condemn; he
claimed authority over the powers of evil as vested, particularly, in Satan; he
claimed to be the Christ or Messiah - a claim which was somehow bound up
with his claim to be the Son of God.[36]

     Yet at the same time as making these stupendous claims about his person
and his authority, Jesus said such things as 'I am gentle and lowly of heart'.[37]
And as for his mission on earth, as soon as his closest followers recognized
and confessed (Peter being their spokesman) that he was truly Messiah and
Son of God, he warned them 'that he must go to Jerusalem and suffer many
things from the elders and chief priests and scribes, and be killed . . .'[38] Such

predictions were reiterated in a variety of ways, including the oblique way of incorporating the prediction in a parable.[39] Though isolated predictions ascribed to Christ about his death may be thought by some to be inventions of Jesus' followers *ex eventu*, it is much more difficult to dismiss such a prediction embedded in a parable recorded by three of the four gospel writers. If any form of teaching is utterly characteristic of Jesus it is his employment of parables; moreover, if any sections of his teaching are likely, after he had left them, to have been recalled by his followers accurately, it is these same parables. The parable in question, that of the wicked husbandmen, is as typical as any. What is more, the prediction of his death in that parable is followed up by a particularly memorable saying underlining the point about his coming rejection. Jesus quotes some words from a psalm: 'The very stone which the builders rejected has become the head of the corner . . .'[40]

So much for what Jesus said about himself before his death. Most significant of all, however, is the fact that - according to the unanimous verdict of the records we have - he accepted death, when it came through the betrayal of a friend, the plottings of enemies, and the weakness of the Roman governor, without making any attempt to resist it. This is the real proof that Jesus had consistently taught his followers that his authority was spiritual rather than political, and that his kingdom was - as he said in answer to Pilate's question - 'not of this world'.[41]

It has been argued that Jesus, by these words 'not of this world', meant no more than that his authority was not derived out of this world, and that he was not speaking about its character in exercise or its sphere of exercise. The argument seems less tenuous if the Greek word *basileia*, normally rendered 'kingdom',[42] is rendered (as in the Revised Standard Version) 'kingship'. This translation seems intended to dilute the plain meaning of the statement in John 18:36 that the kingdom to which Jesus was referring is in some way beyond and quite different in kind from all earthly kingdoms. That the latter interpretation is correct, however, is established beyond doubt by some further words of Jesus which John records. Jesus, we read, tells Pilate that the other-worldly nature of his kingdom is demonstrated by the fact that his servants were not taking up arms to prevent his being handed over to the Jewish authorities. Had his kingdom been of this world, they would have fought, Jesus insists.[43]

Of course, the circumstances of Jesus' death have been disputed. In particular, it has been disputed that Jesus made no attempt to make a bid for political power, or that his servants truly gave no resistance to his arrest. Kahl claims, as we have seen, that the gospel narratives are too unreliable for anything certain about Jesus - and especially his death - to be established. We have, however, discussed the weaknesses of this position, and pointed out that the majority of both Christian and non-Christian scholars consider the records sufficiently accurate to reconstruct what actually happened. We are therefore in a position to consider the general proposal that Jesus was convicted and executed as a political offender, and, further, the suggestion - proposed by Kahl as the last of his three 'unverifiable' explanations as to why Jesus was crucified - that he actually was a political revolutionary.

One of the most scholarly studies of the circumstances of Jesus' death is that published in 1971 by David Catchpole, *The Trial of Jesus*.[44] Catchpole identifies four theories of the way in which events could have led up to Jesus' crucifixion at the hands of the Romans as a political offender.[45]

Firstly, there is the 'misunderstanding theory'. Jesus, a mystic dreamer, claimed messiahship and preached the kingdom of God in a spiritual, non-political sense. The masses were disappointed and politically frustrated, or they simply did not understand. In either case, the Romans considered Jesus politically a menace and took appropriate action. Secondly, we have the 'messianic claim' theory. Jesus claimed messiahship, and did so particularly at the entry to Jerusalem. In varying degrees this is coupled with the view that Jesus aimed to restore national independence, an aim largely erased by the gospels.[46] Thirdly, there is the 'popular unrest' theory. This tones down the political aspects of Jesus' career and argues that it was his effect upon people rather than than any deliberate claims which provoked police action.[47] Political aspirations were present,[48] but there was no messianic claim, not unequivocally even before Pilate.[49] The 'Zealot theory', an extreme version of the 'messianic claim' theory, constitutes the final explanation of Jesus' death as a political offender. Catchpole cites the Jewish writers R. Eisler and J. Carmichael as the clearest modern exponents of this theory, which argues that Jesus was a political revolutionary.

The last of these theories runs as follows: John the Baptist was a Zealot leader, whom Jesus admired, and Jesus' baptism at his hands initiated Jesus into a political association aiming to purify from the cardinal sin of serving the Romans. Jesus at first took a more pacifist line, but, stirred by his own eschatology, and disappointed by his failure in Galilee, he decided to seek a showdown in Jerusalem. When he entered Jerusalem seated on a donkey a few days before the Passover, with the crowds shouting 'Hosanna!' ('Free now!') and waving palm branches, he was in fact leading an armed insurrection. He occupied the Temple by armed force, while supporters seized the tower of Siloam. The rebellion was, however, put down by the Romans who arrested Jesus and had him executed as a rebel.[50]

Catchpole also refers to the non-Jewish writer S.G.F. Brandon, whose argument is similar to that of Eisler and Carmichael at many points.[51] Jesus himself, Brandon proposes, was not a Zealot, but his movement was closely parallel and at times overlapped with Zealot aims and principles.

Catchpole concludes that Brandon's theory 'fails to carry conviction on a number of points'.[52] Brandon argues, for instance, that Zealotry had a theological foundation of zeal for the law and Pharisaism that might have been attractive to Jesus, whose reforming zeal was fundamentally theological; yet Jesus held views that divided him from Pharisaism and precluded total acceptance of the law as interpreted by his contemporaries, and these views would have ruled out his acceptance of Zealotry.[53] Again, there is no hard evidence that Jesus encouraged the idea of an overthrow of the political order, despite what Brandon calls his 'imminent eschatology' and the undoubted fact that Jesus' followers cherished aspirations of national independence.[54] Indeed, as Catchpole points out, Jesus' emphasis on the present process of the kingdom's realization would have been offensive to Zealots whilst the Romans were still in control of the land.[55] Further, the fact that one of the twelve close disciples of Jesus was (or had been) a member of the politically motivated Zealot party[56] only illustrates how widely Jesus' net was cast, to include even those repugnant to both Pharisees and Zealots - the prostitutes and tax-gatherers.[57] We also have the clear testimony of John's gospel to Jesus' refusal to yield to popular pressure to adopt a political role following the feeding of the five thousand,[58] the evidence that Jesus advised the payment of tribute to Caesar[59] (an attitude abhorrent to the Zealots), and the impossibility of attaching to Jesus' action in cleansing the Temple a political motive.[60] Catchpole adduces five other weaknesses in Brandon's thesis, and concludes: 'Jesus was no Zealot, nor was he close to the Zealots. It is altogether in excess of the evidence to regard his movement and Zealotism as parallel or in sympathy with one another.'[61]

There is no reason to believe that Jesus was politically motivated and guilty, in some way, of sedition against Rome, so we can return to the other two possibilities advanced by Kahl as explanations for Jesus' death: that Jesus' death was the necessary conclusion to his opposition to traditional Judaism so that the Jewish authorities had to get rid of him, or that Jesus was executed by the Romans as a messianic prophet because they did not recognize the unpolitical character of his role.

The second of these propositions roughly corresponds to the first of Catchpole's categories - although for Catchpole's category the 'misunderstanding' is located in the Jewish masses rather than the Roman authorities. The proposition can also be linked to Catchpole's third 'popular unrest' category - that Jesus was executed because the Romans were afraid of the disturbing effect He had upon the people.[62]

Since even Jesus' intimate followers misunderstood him,[63] it is obvious that the Jewish masses also failed to appreciate the true nature of his mission.[64] It is not so clear that the Romans, as represented by Pontius Pilate, misunderstood Jesus' role, if the gospel accounts have any veracity; it is to Pilate that Jesus declared that his kingdom was 'not of this world', immediately after which Pilate announced to the Jews 'I find no crime in him.'[65] Pilate's action of 'washing his hands' of responsibility of 'this just person', recorded by Matthew,[66] underlines the fact that Pilate recognized Jesus' innocence under the law. He could not, of course, legitimately abrogate responsibility in the matter, and his decision to order Jesus' crucifixion seems to have been dictated partly by his fear of 'popular unrest' - that is, by the fear that, whatever Jesus' true nature and role, there could be a riot if he did not quickly take action by getting Jesus permanently out of the way.[67] We may also infer from the account in John that Pilate was afraid that the Jewish authorities might, if he released Jesus, make an official complaint that he had been disloyal to Caesar.[68]

There remains the first of Kahl's potential explanations as to the reason for Jesus' death. This is the proposal that, whatever Pilate thought and did, the Jewish leaders were in any case determined to bring about Jesus' death because his teaching was unacceptable to them. A straightforward reading of the gospel accounts does in fact give us such a picture, and it is affirmed by the Jewish writer Hugh Schonfield. His conclusions on this matter are worth recording in full: 'Jesus never said he would fall into the hands of the Jewish people, but into the hands of the chief priests, elders and scribes. The Gospels testify that the commons of the Jewish nation heard him gladly, and that the Council acted secretly without the knowledge of the people, because they feared a popular demonstration by the Jews in Jesus' favour. We have the evidence that they decided on the removal of Jesus in private conclave, and, taking advantage of his betrayal by one of his own disciples, arrested and interrogated him by night so that the Jewish people assembled in their multitudes at Jerusalem for the Passover should be totally ignorant of what was taking place.

'We have already considered the motives of the Council, which in the main were those of self-preservation and self-interest, though not wholly divorced from considerations of national and spiritual survival. These wealthy aristocrats knew they were out of favour with the Jewish masses while they served a foreign heathen government and that their standing with Rome was precarious. Shorn of many of their former powers they were walking a tightrope, clinging to office, inherited prestige and luxurious living, maintaining their position by high-handed action and tortuous intrigue.'[69]

Schonfield, it should be said, insists that there were 'good men among the Jewish leaders, a dissentient minority', and that 'probably some of the Pharisee members of the Council absented themselves from the assembly which dealt with Jesus'.[70] He also argues extenuating circumstances for the Council's generally immoral action by reiterating his central thesis that 'Jesus had deliberately manoeuvred them into the position where they were forced to proceed against him.'[71] But his concession that the Jewish authorities were in many ways grievously at fault is an important and far-reaching one.

That Jesus deliberately engineered his arrest and crucifixion, perhaps even attempting (as Schonfield argues) to stage-manage the semblance of a 'resurrection',[72] is a view that leaves too many questions unanswered. The argument necessitates a cavalier treatment of the gospel records - the selection of certain passages and the ignoring of others - as well as the indulging in a great deal of 'reading between the lines'. We are left, therefore, with a Jesus whose execution followed the machinations of the Jewish authorities and the combined fear and cowardice of the Roman governor.

The figure who stepped so quietly on to the stage of history nearly two thousand years ago most nearly conforms to the kind of person presupposed by the first picture offered by Kahl - a figure whose death was the necessary conclusion to his opposition to traditional Judaism, so that the Jewish authorities had to get rid of him. Catchpole, after his exhaustive examination of all aspects of Jesus' trial, sums up his own verdict in two sentences: 'The one place where Jesus can be shown to have caused offence is in matters religious. It is here he was both different and dangerous, and it would be surprising if his end should take up something he had not done and completely bypass something he had done.'[73]

Jesus had a spiritual message for mankind; it was to commend and to establish a heavenly kingdom that he lived and died.

8
Kingdom and Church

After his resurrection, Jesus gave a charge to to his disciples to take to the whole world the message he had delivered to them.[1]

'After his resurrection', we say - and in so doing beg a question of some moment for those who do not call themselves Christians, as also for some who do.[2]

As already stated, it is not the primary purpose of this book formally to argue the truth of the claims of Christianity. Nevertheless, it should here be pointed out that there are very significant flaws in the arguments put forward by those who wish to dismiss the claim that the dead body of Jesus miraculously disappeared from the tomb in which it had been placed. Various theories have been advanced to provide a natural explanation. Some have suggested, for example, that Jesus never really died, but only swooned on the cross, and revived in the coolness of the tomb.[3] Others, as we have seen, have suggested that the women who went early to embalm Jesus' body went to the wrong tomb.[4] Yet others have proposed that the disciples themselves stole away the body.[5]

Unlikely assumptions have to be made in order to sustain the above suggestions, not least the psychological difficulty of believing that the early disciples were able - without irrefutable evidence of the truth of Jesus' resurrection - to preach, convince others about, and die for, such an astonishing and improbable story. The disciples' claim to have met Jesus in risen form after his death refers, of course, to the most obvious form of evidence available for the truth of his divine nature and his message.[6] Yet it would be a mistake to underestimate the significance, for those early disciples, of the disappearance of Jesus' body from the tomb. It is clear, from the gospel accounts, that in some ways this was a corner-stone of belief for the first disciples.[7]

Perhaps the simplest form of argument for the truth of Christianity is that first set forth by St Augustine of Hippo, and which boils down to the proposition that the extreme egocentricity and potential blasphemy of the claims Jesus made - that of possessing divine attributes, like the right to forgive sins and to judge men in an ultimate sense - mean that only three possible statements about him can be made: either he was wicked, or he was deranged, or he was what he claimed to be.[8] In fact, in view of the depth and wisdom of his ethical teaching, virtually no one has tried to suggest that Jesus was bad; and the charge that he was deranged is usually muted. He is sometimes described as having been 'mistaken', notwithstanding the fact that the serious claim by a human to be divine is usually considered to be a sure sign of insanity. More often recourse is had to the argument that Jesus himself never actually made the claim to divinity; the New Testament, it is argued, is in this respect a fabrication of second-generation Christians. But such an argument does insufficient justice, as we have seen in the previous chapter, to the evidence for the reliability of our sources.

On the assumption that Jesus was what he claimed to be, let us turn to a consideration of the gospel, or good news, of the kingdom - in the teaching of Jesus, in the experience of the first Christians, in the teaching of other New Testament writers.

A Kingdom on earth: the Church's birth, and conditions of entry
Who exactly were and are the members of Jesus' kingdom, and how is membership achieved?

It was to the very first members of his kingdom, the first disciples, that Jesus gave the final charge recorded in Matthew's gospel. At that time, however, though members, they were not participating fully in the privileges of membership. Luke tells us that part of the final charge was to wait. Not until they had received 'the promise of my Father', and were 'clothed with power from on high' were they to be 'witnesses in Jerusalem and in all Judea and Samaria and to the end of the earth'.[9]

The fulfilment of this promise of the Father was to be the seal of membership, and an empowering for the task ahead. It was also to indicate the nature of the body which those first disciples were joining.

It was at the Jewish feast of Pentecost that some kind of supernatural event is recorded as having occurred.[10] Christians have always believed it to have been the entering of Christ's own spirit into the hearts and minds and spirits of his first followers. Jesus had earlier said that he was going, after his departure, to send 'another Counsellor, to be with you for ever, even the Spirit of truth'.[11]

After that memorable Pentecost the first Christians were transformed. In the Acts of the Apostles, written by the author of the third Gospel, we find that it was following their experience on that Jewish feast-day that the disciples of Jesus began fearlessly to preach the bodily resurrection of Jesus from the dead, together with his divinity and, of course, messiahship.[12] Many others believed as a result of this initial preaching, and were baptized;[13] and from that time there was a steady increase in the membership of the fledgling Church.[14]

So the Church had her birth, a supernatural birth - and an outpost of the kingdom of heaven was established on earth. In this outpost the kingdom was to exist solely in the hearts of its members; it was (and is, in fact) the realm of the Spirit - the 'Counsellor' or 'Spirit of truth'. That Spirit, Jesus made it clear, was the Spirit of himself and his Father, for he immediately followed up the promise of the coming of the 'Counsellor' with the words: 'I will not leave you desolate; I will come to you . . . In that day you will know that I am in the Father, and you in me, and I in you . . . If a man loves me, he will keep my word, and my Father will love him, and we will come to him and make our home with him.'[15]

What had qualified those first Christians for membership of this new community, for this indwelling of the Spirit? The fact that they were Jews? The fact that they had known Jesus in the flesh, or seen him after his resurrection? The fact that they had passed some test - intellectual or moral? No. The Spirit entered those first Christians because they loved Jesus.

When we love someone we do so spontaneously. Indeed, love which is not spontaneous is no true love. You cannot manufacture love; it is an instinctive response to beauty - physical love is a response to physical beauty, spiritual love is a response to spiritual, or moral, beauty. And the spiritual beauty of Jesus has elicited just such a spontaneous love from men and women of all ages, of all climes, of all races. This, ultimately, is the single condition for entry into the new spiritual community which is the Church of Jesus. It is the response of a man's heart, of his desires - not his intellect, or even, ultimately, his will. What is important is what a man *wants*, not what he has done, or can by nature or training make himself do; for, in any case, as Jesus also said, 'apart from me you can do nothing'.[16]

Those who love Jesus, we read, keep his word. It is the love, however, which is prior, not the obedience; and where love is present, obedience is bound to follow. 'Lord, you know everything; you know that I love you,' responded Peter to Jesus - and was given a command to obey.[17]

For acceptance into the new community there must, of course, be a willingness to put aside known sin; there must be repentance. In what is perhaps the most beautiful and moving story Jesus ever told, the parable of the prodigal son, this is emphasized. After he had squandered all his property in loose living, and been reduced to being a swineherd, the son finally came to himself and returned to his father with the words, 'Father, I have sinned against heaven and before you; I am no longer worthy to be called your son.'[18] The repentance was there - but nothing more. He could offer nothing from his past, only his wasted life. But the father's acceptance was there too; the erring son was immediately received back, being given all the privileges of sonship.

Repentance always has to be present for any relationship to be restored between a person wronged, and the wrongdoer. This is as true between God and man as it is between man and his brother. But repentance, of course, is simply a corollary of love. The other corollary of love is trust - faith, or belief.

'Believe me that I am in the Father and the Father in me,' Jesus said to Philip.[19] That was to one who had already responded to him. But he said the same to all. The people who lived on the far side of the Lake of Tiberias, who followed after him when he had refused to allow them 'to make him king', asked him, 'What must we do, to be doing the work of God?' They were asking the fundamental question: what is required of those who would be members of Jesus' kingdom? His reply was simple: 'This is the work of God, that you believe in him whom he has sent.' When they pressed him to prove by a 'sign' that he was sent by God, asking 'What work do you perform?', he expanded on this original reply: 'I am the bread of life; he who comes to me shall not hunger, and he who believes in me shall never thirst . . . this is the will of my Father, that every one who sees the Son and believes in him should have eternal life; and I will raise him up at the last day.'[20]

Christians, therefore, are those who love Jesus, and who, because they love him, keep his word - believe in him, have faith in him, follow him.[21] The supreme significance of faith, expounded so fully by St Paul in his letters, is the truth which was largely lost for a millenium, once Christianity had become a state religion, until it was rediscovered and proclaimed by Martin Luther.

Jesus had talked about establishing a kingdom of heaven, of which he was leader. The new community of believers in him - for whom was fulfilled on that day of Pentecost the promise he had given them, a new and spiritual birth - constituted an outpost of the kingdom on earth. Subsequent believers in Jesus, all of whom have shared in the gift of God's indwelling Spirit, have, to this day, constituted a continuing outpost of that kingdom.

The Church's nature

If the Church's birth was spiritual, and if her continued existence was and is dependent upon the spiritual birth of each new believer, what further can we say about her nature?

There are three important images in the New Testament used to describe the Church, and thus to depict her true nature. The first is the image represented by the very word 'church' itself.

The English word 'church' translates a Greek word *ekklesia*. The word is a noun from the verb *ekkaleo*, which means 'to call out', or 'to summon forth'.[22] Jesus did not often use the word, insofar as we can tell this from the gospels. In fact it is only in Matthew's gospel that we find the word ascribed to Jesus. There is the famous occasion on which Jesus told Peter that 'upon this rock' (Peter's confession of faith, presumably) 'I will build my church'; and there is the occasion on which Jesus tells his disciples what to do when a 'brother' sins against them.[23] However, the term is used regularly in the Acts of the Apostles, in the Epistles, and in the book of Revelation, to describe the body of Christian believers.

Christians, we must understand from this word *ekklesia*, are a people who have been 'called out'. This idea is, in Acts, used by the apostle James, a leading figure in the early Jerusalem church, when the question arose as to whether the Church should fully accept new members from amongst the Gentiles. Referring to the testimony of Simon Peter, who as well as Paul and Barnabas had preached to and baptized Gentiles, James says: 'Simeon has related how God first visited the Gentiles, to take out of them a people for his name.'[24] The idea is simple: the Church is a body of people which has been extracted, or rescued (hence the regular use in Acts and elsewhere of the term 'saved' and 'salvation' to describe the Christians' status),[25] from the mass of mankind. It is the idea which Jesus expressed when he said to his disciples in the upper room just before his death: 'If you were of the world, the world would love its own; but because you are not of the world, but I chose you out of the world, therefore the world hates you.'[26] The fact of being called, taken, chosen 'out of' the world does not mean, Jesus elsewhere makes very clear, that his followers are to become a band of solitaries, having no dealings with the world at all. 'I do not pray,' he addressed his Father on that same occasion, 'that thou shouldst take them out of the world, but that thou shouldst keep them from the evil one. They are not of the world, even as I am not of the world.'[27] So - as we so often say - the Church is to be 'in the world, but not of it'.

For the world, according to Jesus, is still in some strange permissive sense the realm and possession of Satan. We have already seen this from the account of Jesus' temptations.[28] It is also apparent from the appeal of the demoniacs to be cast into the swine.[29] John records that Jesus calls Satan 'the ruler of this world.'[30] The idea is made even more explicit in the third epistle of John, which was probably written by the author of John's gospel:[31] 'We know that we are of God, and the whole world is in the power of the evil one.'[32]

The body of Christian believers, therefore, is an entity which, though it has a role in this world, is nevertheless quite distinct from it. It is unique on the earth; it is quite different from all other associations of people in the world..

This brings us to the second New Testament image used to describe the Church's nature. It is the image presented by the apostle Paul in describing the Church as the body of Christ.

There is nothing incongruous about this image. As we have already seen, the Church's birth was spiritual. This means that her very nature is spiritual. She is not an organization as other human associations are organizations; rather is she an *organism*. Human organizations have a physical life in the sense that they are formed from physically living individuals. The Church, however, is alive in a different sense. She is spiritually alive because her members are all filled with the Spirit of Jesus - God himself, the Spirit of God.[33] It is in the light of this fact that Paul can describe the Church as a living body, with Jesus Christ himself as Head.[34]

Paul vividly depicts the spiritual relationship of the Church with her Head in a passage from his letter to the Colossians. Christians, he warns, must not neglect to hold fast 'to the Head, from whom the whole body, nourished and knit together through its joints and ligaments, grows with a growth which is from God'.[35]

But where is this Head? He is not, like the chairman of an earthly organization, presiding visibly over his 'body'. No. The Church's Head, Jesus Christ, is only invisibly present on the earth. In a bodily sense (that resurrected body which the first Christians claimed to have seen over a period of forty days)[36], he lives in a heavenly sphere - a different dimension, if you like, for which the inadequate term 'above' is the best that everyday human language can manage. Following on from his exhortation to Christians about 'holding fast to the Head', Paul refers to this truth of Christ's heavenly existence. Indeed, he argues from this fact that Christians should in a spiritual, if not bodily, sense also inhabit that heavenly realm. 'If then you have been raised with Christ,' he exhorts his readers, 'seek those things that are above, where Christ is, seated at the right hand of God. Set your minds on things that are above, not on things that are on the earth. For you have died, and your life is hid with Christ in God. When Christ, who is our life, appears, then you also will appear with him in glory.'[37]

The true home of Christians, he is saying, is not on earth at all; it is in heaven. On earth, as the writer of the letter to the Hebrews has it, we are to follow the example of believers of Old Testament times, who, living by faith ('the assurance of things hoped for, the conviction of things not seen')[38] 'acknowledged that they were strangers and exiles on the earth'; they desired 'a better country, that is, a heavenly one'.[39]

All this - the fact of Christ's invisible Headship of the Church, the fact that the life of Christians is 'hid with Christ in God', the fact that Christians live by faith, the fact that Christians are to 'desire a better country, that is, a heavenly one' - is what led Luther to make his protest, the crucial assertion, that Christ is the only Head of the Church, which is invisible, known only to God. It is this truth, one that he first learnt from St Augustine, which was the foundation-stone of Luther's protest, for it cut through the arguments of those who wished the ordinary Christian to submit to the dictates of a worldly ecclesiastical hierarchy, and who claimed that the Church had divine authority to rule in the secular sphere. The question of the Church's real nature remains today the fundamental matter to which Christians should address themselves as they seek to identify the Church's role in the world.

The third image used in the New Testament to describe the Church is one that probably came from Jesus. This is the image of marriage: the Church is a bride, Jesus is the bridegroom.

Three of the gospels - the 'synoptic' gospels, Matthew, Mark and Luke - record an incident in which the disciples of John the Baptist came to Jesus with a question about fasting; they were accustomed to fast regularly, whereas the disciples of Jesus did not fast. Jesus gave this answer: 'Can the wedding guests mourn as long as the bridegroom is with them? The days will come, when the bridegroom is taken away from them, and then they will fast.'[40] Jesus here pictures himself as a bridegroom, though his disciples are 'wedding guests', not grouped collectively as 'the bride'. For the point he was making at the time, it would not, of course, have been very helpful to picture his disciples in the latter fashion. The same is true for the one other occasion in the synoptic gospels when Jesus likens himself to a bridegroom - the parable of the five wise, and five foolish, virgins.[41] In John's gospel, however, the image of Jesus as bridegroom is used by John the Baptist, and here it is a 'bride' who is the counterpart to Jesus. John the Baptist is disclaiming any title to messiahship, and does so by likening himself to the 'bridegroom's friend', whilst Jesus is the bridegroom, who 'has the bride'.[42] It seems likely that John used this metaphor because Jesus had already used it; Jesus' answer to John's disciples had, in fact, probably been passed on to John. What is significant is the fact that John's reference to the bride was not strictly necessary for the main point he was making, which was that Jesus, not himself, was the key figure. 'The bride' must therefore have meant something like the kingdom of which Jesus was ruler, and which he had come to establish. That kingdom, we have seen, was and is a kingdom of men's hearts, a kingdom represented from that time until now by the Church. Perhaps Jesus had himself, in John's presence, talked of his kingdom as his 'bride'.

Elsewhere in the New Testament we find Paul using the analogy of a husband and wife, or a betrothed couple, for Christ's relationship with the Church.[43] He seems at one point to be thinking in terms of the arrival of the bride at a marriage ceremony, for he writes that 'Christ loved the church, and gave himself up for her . . . that he might present the church to himself in splendour, without spot or wrinkle or any such thing, that she might be holy and without blemish.'[44] It is in the book of Revelation, however, that the image of the Church as Christ's bride is clearest: ' ". . . the marriage of the Lamb has come, and his Bride has made herself ready; it was granted her to be clothed with fine linen, bright and pure" - for the fine linen is the righteous deeds of the saints.'[45]

That marriage is to take place in heaven.

A *heavenly destiny*

So the Church's destiny is a *heavenly* one; it is that of a perfect union with her bridegroom or - to revert to the earlier metaphor - a perfect union of the body of Christ with its Head. This destiny, this future goal, is where the Church should be looking.

Some of the last words in the book of Revelation, and therefore in the Bible, are these: 'The Spirit and the Bride say, "Come".'[46] The Spirit who indwells every Christian believer, who indwells, that is, the true but invisible Church, is looking and longing for the consummation, the marriage, and the

Bride can only articulate the Spirit's yearning. This heavenly consummation is the hope of the Church, the hope of every Christian. The cry is 'Come', and the one who is to come is the bridegroom, Jesus - the Lamb, the Lord, in glory. 'For', as Paul puts it, 'the Lord himself will descend from heaven with a cry of command, with the archangel's call, and with the sound of the trumpet of God. And the dead in Christ will rise first; then we who are alive, who are left, shall be caught up together with them in the clouds to meet the Lord in the air; and so we shall always be with the Lord. Therefore comfort one another with these words.'[47] 'I tell you a mystery,' he explains elsewhere. 'We shall not all sleep, but we shall all be changed, in a moment, in the twinkling of an eye, at the last trumpet.'[48] 'When Christ who is our life appears,' we have already read from his letter to the Colossians, 'then you also will appear with him in glory.'[49]

This great message of comfort and hope for the Church emanates, of course, from Jesus himself: 'Let not your hearts be troubled; believe in God, believe also in me. In my Father's house are many rooms; if it were not so, would I have told you that I go to prepare a place for you? And when I go and prepare a place for you, I will come again and will take you to myself, that where I am you may be also.'[50] 'Behold, the bridegroom! Come out to meet him.'[51] 'Watch therefore, for you do not know on what day your Lord is coming.'[52]

'I will come again.'

Do we hear this from our pulpits? Do we read about this in Christian magazines and newspapers? Is this the message with which leading Christian pastors comfort and inspire Christians who look to them for counsel? Such teaching is incorporated into our liturgies, and we hear the words read from the lectern, especially at funeral services, but it is usually without a word of exposition. The massive silence that surrounds the doctrine within the churches tells its own story.

The world-centred character of today's institutional churches is only too evident, and has been amply demonstrated. What matters in today's Church is - in the words of Bishop David Jenkins, when challenged about his assertion that Christ's ascension was 'obviously a built-up story' - the 'working here on earth of heavenly things'.[53]

Indeed and indeed, the 'working here on earth of heavenly things' is important, but such work is most effectively promoted when the reality of heavenly things, and the heavenly destiny of heaven's servants, is recognized and proclaimed, not muted or distorted. The most heavenly minded - from Jesus onwards - have always been the most earthly use.

Do we properly understand what it is that the Church should be seeking to accomplish on earth in heaven's name? That is the crucial question. Yet vast numbers of professing Christians are so busily engaged in worldly work of every description that the question is seldom asked, let alone answered.

Jesus both embodied and preached about a kingdom whose nature was non-worldly, spiritual. Those who love him, who believe and trust in him, are its present embodiment on earth. That kingdom we now call the Church - a called-out assembly. The categories constantly reiterated by Jesus in his teaching, as also subsequently by his followers - sin, repentance, faith, forgiveness, baptism, rebirth in the Spirit, resurrection - apply to individuals, not to society as a whole.

Jesus' final charge to the first members of the Church was unambiguous: 'Go therefore and make disciples of all nations, baptizing them in the name of the Father and of the Son and of the Holy Spirit, teaching them to observe all that I have commanded you; and lo, I am with you always, to the close of the age.'[54] The single commission given by Jesus to his Church is the proclamation to all mankind of the Gospel; it is the commending, by word or deed, of the good news of forgiveness and eternal life - that heavenly destiny made possible for all men by what Jesus achieved through his death and resurrection. In a word, the task of the Church in relation to the world in this age is evangelism.

9

God and Caesar

The two contexts

The Church is a Spirit-filled community of people; her nature is spiritual, her task evangelism.

If these things are so, what is the Church's proper stance in relation to the world, the secular sphere? To answer this question adequately we need to look more closely at the way in which the Church functions. As a spiritual entity, distinct from the world at large, the Church has her own way of doing things - her own norms, or ground-rules. These are quite distinct from that which appertains in the world at large.

It is sometimes claimed that a form of communism should be normative for the Christian community, on the basis of its adoption by the first Jewish Christians, as recorded in Acts.[1] The practice, however, is nowhere stated in the New Testament to be mandatory for Christians; indeed, it is clear that Peter, though he no doubt supported this early Christian collectivism, considered that it was *not* mandatory.[2] It appears to have been an experiment which was in due course largely abandoned as impracticable.

Other distinctive patterns of conduct are, however, laid down by the New Testament as normative for Christians, and the question of discipline within the Church provides a notable example of such a norm.

The Church, unlike the the kingdoms of this world, has no sanction to impose on her members besides that of dismissal from active membership of the community. Where a member of the Church has sinned, every effort is made to show him the error of his ways, but if he persists in his sin, he is excommunicated. That is Jesus' own teaching: 'If your brother sins against you, go and tell him his fault, between you and him alone. If he listens to you, you have gained your brother. But if he does not listen, take one or two others along with you, that every word may be confirmed by the evidence of two or three witnesses. If he refuses to listen to them, tell it to the church; and if he refuses to listen even to the church, let him be to you as a Gentile and a tax collector.'[3] St Paul later reiterates this principle of excommunication for those who persist in sinful behaviour.[4]

Jesus' teaching on excommunication implies that between Christians there can be no question of litigation; and on another occasion he counsels out-of-court settlements, and the refusal to challenge those who bring a case

73

against you.[5] St Paul continues in the same vein: 'When one of you has a grievance against a brother, does he dare go to law before the unrighteous instead of the saints? . . . Can it be that there is no man among you wise enough to decide between members of the brotherhood, but brother goes to law against brother, and that before unbelievers? To have lawsuits at all with one another is defeat for you. Why not rather suffer wrong? Why not rather be defrauded?'[6]

This ruling that Christians should not go to court with one another is, of course, merely an extension of the general principle not to resist evil. 'Do not resist one who is evil,' Jesus teaches, 'but if any one strikes you on the right cheek, turn to him the other also.'[7] These are, of course, the ethics of perfection. Jesus, indeed, concludes his teaching about non-resistance to evil with the injunction, 'You, therefore, must be perfect, as your heavenly Father is perfect.'[8] The Church, the community of Christian believers, is in fact required to reflect the ideal of perfection. The Church, as we have seen, is an outpost of the kingdom of heaven, and in heaven life is unsullied perfection. Just as the Church's Head, Jesus, lived a life of perfection on earth, and just as he suffered unjustly, refusing to use force to protect his interests or the interests of his kingdom, so Christians should be prepared to suffer unjustly for the sake of that kingdom, and for the sake of its King.[9]

Within the context of the kingdom of heaven, within the context, that is, of the Church, and where the interests of that kingdom or Church are at stake, the ethics of perfection must be upheld. Luther realized this, as we have seen from what he said about fighting for the Church reforms he wanted: 'I do not wish to do battle for the gospel with force and slaughter. The world is overcome by the Word.'[10] The kingdom of heaven cannot be extended, or defended, by the sword; indeed, the use of force and coercion of any kind is totally out of place where the interests of Christ's kingdom are concerned. The kingdom of heaven is extended, and its interests are preserved, solely through the power of the Spirit who dwells within each member of that kingdom. The Christian battle is spiritual, and the weapons used on its behalf must be spiritual. 'We are not contending against flesh and blood, but against . . . the spiritual hosts of wickedness in the heavenly places . . . Therefore take the whole armour of God . . . truth . . . the breastplate of righteousness . . . the gospel of peace . . . the shield of faith . . . the helmet of salvation . . . the sword of the Spirit, which is the word of God.'[11]

This kingdom of heaven, the kingdom of Christ, of which all Christians are members, must not be confused with the kingdoms of this world. Where the latter legitimately have their earthly rulers, their judiciary, their police, their armies, to ensure that peace and justice are maintained within their borders, or that foreign aggressors are repelled, the former can only defend or further its interests by the power of example, persuasion, and prayer. 'Pray at all times in the Spirit,' Paul continues, after his enumeration of the Christian's spiritual weapons.[12] Prayer, which changes things, and can sometimes work miracles, is the first and last resort of the members of Christ's kingdom; law enforcement and war is the last resort, if not the first, of the members of the kingdoms of this world. Not that Christians, members of Christ's kingdom, are themselves perfect, or anything like it. It is simply that, as those reborn or regenerate in God's Spirit, Christians have to conduct themselves within the context of Christ's kingdom, and when acting on its behalf, as if they were currently living in that environment of perfection to which they aspire. However, outside the realm of Christ's kingdom, and within the context of the unregenerate world, another way has to be followed if there is not to be a breakdown of order and justice.

All of which underlines a simple fact about the Church in her relation to the affairs of the world, to the socio-political sphere: the question of her corporate involvement in the world's secular life should not arise; if it does, we have failed to recognize the Church's true nature.

The Church, properly understood, *cannot* enter the socio-political sphere. The world's nature is physical, and it has to use physical tools and weapons. The Church's nature is spiritual, and she uses spiritual tools and weapons. The two realms are, literally, worlds apart.

Living in two realms

Jesus made explicit reference to the two worlds - the two realms or contexts for action. When the Pharisees and Herodians attempted to trap him into committing himself on the question of paying taxes to Caesar, he made the famous reply: 'Render to Caesar the things that are Caesar's, and to God the things that are God's.'[13] And it is this answer of his that gives the clue as to how the individual Christian should conduct himself in the world. For Jesus' answer makes it clear (as he demonstrated also by his teaching and action in other contexts) that there is no question of a Christian opting out of secular society. Christians are not called, as the Christian ascetics thought, to ostracize the world and its systems. On the contrary, they are told that they must work in the world (or they cannot eat), that they must pay tribute to whomsoever it is due, and that they must honour and serve the secular authorities in all things lawful.[14]

How are Christians, who recognize and attempt to adhere to the demands of the kingdom of heaven, to relate to the secular sphere, and its demands?

Not long ago Lord Hailsham wrote an article in the *Baptist Times* in which he stated that the Church and State have to operate in different, though overlapping, spheres, because they deal with different sets of values. 'The Church', he said, 'operates on the conscience of the individual and presupposes his free will. The State is in the business of sticks and carrots. Therefore, it has to impose a different set of values from the Church . . . The State has to justify what it is doing in the light of the fact that it is treating the human being as a donkey.'[15]

/

What is the 'set of values' that the State has to apply, and is it acceptable to the Christian citizen as he seeks to serve both God and Caesar within the context of the State?

The clue to a legitimate involvement in politics by the Christian lies in the recognition of a natural morality, a natural perception of the law of God, enabling Christians to stand together with non-Christians.[16] There are certain moral absolutes upon which all men agree. And though they do not always agree about the occasions on which those absolutes are infringed, they do agree that if they are infringed certain consequences should follow. It is not necessary to set down in detail what this natural morality comprises, but it certainly includes a recognition of such evils as theft (which could include adultery), deceit, gratuitous violence (which includes rape, murder, and exploitation of the weak), the denial of the right to believe (though not necessarily to propagate) what appeals to you, and finally the incitement of others towards the committing of such crimes. It usually includes, too, a recognition of the fact that all men have an equal potential for evil. Those of religious traditions other than the Christian tradition, as well as those of no religion at all, are normally ready to agree on these things, and to co-operate in the task of seeing that such evils are kept to a minimum by a system of civil law enforcement - the 'stick' referred to by Lord Hailsham.

What of the carrot?

The *carrot* is not in essence different from the *stick*. It is simply another means of keeping a check on man's potential for evil. Man, who is naturally selfish, will not automatically put himself out for the common good, but he may be induced to do so if there is the chance of some material reward.

In this the State's task of using sticks and carrots in order to try to ensure the maximum good of each of its individual members, the Christian can co-operate without any sense of abandoning the fulfilment of his duty to God. For one thing, he has Christ's authority for so doing, since Jesus, by paying tribute to Rome, as well as by accepting Rome's verdict on himself, clearly accepted the legitimacy of Caesar's domain, and in consequence the means - like taxation, law enforcement, penal justice, the use of armies - that it is required to adopt.

But the Christian should realize that in the end there is no contradiction between these 'two moralities', the 'natural' level of moral conduct appropriate for the kingdoms of this world and the 'spiritual', or 'Christian', level appropriate for the kingdom of heaven.[17] They appear different because the one is conditional, presupposing an evil environment in which there is sometimes a moral obligation to choose a less than ideal course of action, a 'lesser of evils', and the other is absolute, requiring actions that never fall short of the ideal which would be normative in a perfect environment. Both, however, can be held to proceed from a single definition of love. It is the context that determines the difference. Alan Richardson makes this point clearly: 'There is no such thing as a distinctively Christian moral system. Doubtless moral codes for the instruction of Christians are good and necessary in particular ages; the law of love needs to be spelt out in specific social contexts . . . There is strictly no such thing as Christian ethics, because what is called the Christian ethic is really right human behaviour *qua* human and *qua* universal. Good action is good only if it is good for all men everywhere, the good which the sensitive human conscience universally recognizes, even while admitting that this is a standard beyond human reach.'[18]

The perennial difficulty for the Christian living within secular society is that of knowing when to act in his capacity as a Christian, as a member of the kingdom of heaven, and when to act in his capacity as an earthly citizen, as a member of a kingdom of this world. For instance, the Christian policemen (and we are all to some extent policemen, for we all have citizens' powers of arrest) is clearly going wrong if he 'turns the other cheek' when being attacked by a violent criminal. Though he may even find it in his heart to love his attacker, he must arrest him - perhaps having to use considerable pain-inducing force to do so. It is not his moral duty at that moment to shame the criminal into repentance by a policy of non-retaliation. His duty is to protect himself as an agent of society, to restrain and apprehend the violent man, and in so doing protect society as a whole. Yet there are, no doubt, occasions when that same policemen (or civilian) may judge it right not to retaliate to some personal abuse or even to an attack. It all depends upon the context.

Christians actually inhabit two worlds, and it is not always easy for the Christian to know, at a given moment, which of the two worlds has the prior claim on him. Yet as long as he remembers that it is, ultimately, as we have seen, the law of love that is operating in both spheres, he will not go far wrong. For love will tell him when, in defence of himself or of the kingdom of heaven, he must suffer evil unresistingly; and love it is that will tell him when, for the sake of others - for society, in fact - he must take action himself to restrain evil, using some kind and degree of force, or must ask or allow society's appointed agents to use it on his behalf.[19]

It is the constraint of love, too, which will compel the Christian in a secular society - in his capacity as a citizen, and accepting the moral limitations of unregenerate man - to work towards making the structures of that society more humane and just, as well as more efficient. He will have before him the inspiration of such men as William Wilberforce and Martin Luther King,[20] and, in performing this task, will be making his proper contribution, together with all men of goodwill, towards the establishment of a peaceful and prosperous society, one in which the physical, mental and spiritual welfare of all men is adequately cared for.

A disastrous confusion

What has gone wrong with the Church in the last hundred years or so is that the two kingdoms have become confused. The kingdom of heaven has been construed as a kingdom of this world; the Gospel has been interpreted politically. It is a *social* gospel that Christ delivered to his first disciples, we are told; or, if he did not, he should have done, so a new dimension is added to the New Testament Gospel, because God, as Bishop David Jenkins tells us, is 'also known in and through the contemporary'.[21] This process of reinterpreting the Gospel has already been traced in Part I, Chapter 6. Here it remains to isolate and emphasize the fundamental theological error that lies behind the idea of a social gospel.

The error is what has usually been described in Christian circles as 'universalism'. This is the view that men are sons of God, that they can consider God to be their Father, and can therefore share in all the promises related to this privileged status without the need for repentance from sin and faith in Jesus Christ, and without the need for rebirth in God's Spirit. The theologians perpetrating this error have formed something of a line of succession; here we will summarize the way this happened.

The process began in earnest with the philosophical idealism of S.T. Coleridge, an idealism he owed, in some measure, to that of the utopianist agnostic, Robert Owen. Next in line of succession was F.D. Maurice, who taught explicitly that all men are, by natural birth, not rebirth in the Spirit, under the Headship of Christ. After Maurice came B.F. Westcott, who further fostered the idea that 'all men are brethren in Christ', under the 'present and abiding fatherhood of God.' 'The thoughts of a true socialism,' he wrote, 'the thoughts that men are "one man" in Christ, sons of God and brethren . . . are fundamental thoughts of the Law and the Prophets, of the Gospels and the Epistles . . . We are required to bring the doctrine of the Incarnation to bear upon the dealings of man with man, and of nation with nation'.[22] Westcott's views, and in particular his universalist error, were to greatly influence the thought of Archbishop William Temple, who, as we have seen, once wrote: 'God . . . is the Father of all men' and 'each man . . . is a child of God.'[23]

In our own era, two Anglican bishops of great gifts and immense influence, Trevor Huddleston and David Sheppard, have effectively - if perhaps unconsciously - argued from the same universalist assumption in identifying and opposing socio-political injustices on the grounds that they constitute a 'denial of the Gospel', or are 'un-Christian'. In perhaps his most famous book, *Naught for Your Comfort*, Huddleston writes: 'Young Africa stands waiting . . . we have told him that he is the child of God and an inheritor of the Kingdom of Heaven . . .'[24] One other modern, and comprehensive, statement of this fundamental error will suffice. The Bishop of Manchester, the Right Reverend Stanley Booth-Clibborn, said the following when preaching to the Church Missionary Society in 1973: '. . . the emphasis in the

New Testament on equality in the body of Christ and sharing together in his promise is a challenge . . . Words on all men as sharing in the promise of Christ have profound implications . . . What does it mean to proclaim the Good News and a sharing in the promise of Christ to a world of gross and growing inequalities both within and between nations?' He answered his own question: 'The spiritual dynamic which treats all men of all races as sharers in the promise and members of one body, can also be expressed in economic life . . . so this element in the Gospel is coming to the fore once more - the challenge to a radical reshaping of economic life.' He then called for the churches to be more 'committed politically', suggesting that the Society's members support certain political objectives which 'may well be the real implications of a Gospel which speaks of men as "sharers in the promise" '. Objectives, or 'points in political programmes', which he specified were 'high taxation for the well-off, increased public expenditure in needy areas of the national life, comprehensive education, and a wealth tax'.[25]

Not all advocates of a 'social gospel' fall into the error of 'universalism', explicitly or implicitly, but they tend to build on the theology of those who do, while forgetting the original false premise. Attempts have been made - by Karl Barth, for instance - to 'marry' the two realms, the kingdoms of this world and the kingdom of heaven, arguing that they are, or should somehow be, analogous.[26] This is sometimes done, as by William Temple in his *Christianity and Social Order*, by inventing a kind of social limbo, hovering between the world as it is and the world as it should be. This is Temple's 'Natural Order', which does less than justice to the sinfulness of mankind which the law of God reveals.[27] David Sheppard's book, *Built as a City*, is based upon a similar misapprehension.[28] The wish is to outline a socio-political programme on the basis, to a greater or lesser extent, of the ethics of perfection appropriate within or on behalf of the kingdom of heaven.

Of course, if more and more members of society become Christian, then society can become more like the heavenly ideal. But the horse must come before the cart. You need more individual Christians, more people filled with the heavenly Spirit, before you can have a more heavenly form of society - and you cannot make Christians by legislation. We should remind ourselves, too, that the appealing sentiment of the famous hymn - 'Thy Kingdom stands, and grows for ever, Till all Thy creatures own Thy sway' - is not what Jesus himself taught about the future of the Church and the world. Though many Christians still appear to believe that their efforts, and the efforts of others, will result in continuous moral as well as scientific progress for the world as the future unrolls, the picture of the future consistently painted by Jesus is (if we are to trust the records) utterly different. He gives us a scenario in which 'because wickedness is multiplied, most men's love will grow cold', one in which there will be 'distress of nations in perplexity . . . men fainting with fear and with foreboding of what is coming on the world'.[29] We do not, because of this, give up trying to make our own corner of the world provisionally·a holier and happier place, but we are simply foolish if we ignore what Jesus has told us.

Let us return to the question of who - according to the New Testament, rather than to those advocating a 'social gospel' - are 'in Christ', who are 'sharers in the promise', and who have God as 'Father'. In answering the question I shall, of course, be amplifying only what was written in the last chapter about who are the members of Jesus' kingdom, the Church.

The New Testament makes it quite clear that all men everywhere are *potentially* able to enjoy these privileges. But it is that crucial word 'potentially' that is omitted by the exponents of Christian Socialism we have cited. Paul is the great New Testament exponent of how someone becomes a sharer in Christ's promises. In his letter to the Ephesian Christians, he says: 'You also, who have . . . believed in him, were sealed with the promised Holy Spirit'.[30] To the Galatians he writes: 'The scripture consigned all things to sin, that what was promised to faith in Jesus Christ might be given to those who believe . . . for in Christ Jesus you are all sons of God, through faith. For as many of you as were baptized into Christ have put on Christ . . . you are all one in Christ Jesus . . . heirs according to promise . . . I mean that the heir, as long as he is a child, is no better than a slave . . . So with us . . . we were slaves to the elemental spirits of the universe. But when the time had fully come, God sent forth his Son . . . so that we might receive adoption as sons. And because you are sons, God has sent forth the Spirit of his Son into our hearts, crying, "Abba! Father!"'[31]

It is 'to those who believe' that 'what was promised in Christ Jesus might be given'. It is 'through faith' that men are 'in Christ Jesus' and 'sons of God'. It is those who have been 'baptized into Christ' who have 'put on Christ', who have received 'adoption as sons' and can therefore call God 'Abba! Father!' Men become sons of God, they can claim him as Father, only by a process of *adoption*; by natural birth they do not enjoy that status. They are by nature God's creatures, but they are not by nature his sons. By nature they are 'slaves to the elemental spirits of the universe', and these spirits are demonic. They are 'the principalities . . . the powers . . . the world rulers of this present darkness . . . the spiritual hosts of wickedness in the heavenly places.'[32] And, Paul tells Christians, 'you were dead through the trespasses and sins in which you once walked, following the course of this world, following the prince of the power of the air, the spirit that is now at work in the sons of disobedience. Among these we all once lived in the passions of our flesh, following the desires of body and mind, and so we were by nature children of wrath, like the rest of mankind'.[33] God, however, as a result of our 'faith in Christ Jesus', has 'delivered us from the dominion of darkness and transferred us to the kingdom of his beloved Son, in whom we have redemption, the forgiveness of sins.'[34]

Paul was only following the teaching of Jesus, of course, for Jesus, as we have seen, made it no less clear that membership of his kingdom and enjoyment of the attendant blessings were conditional - that faith, or belief in him, was a prerequisite. To Nicodemus he put it slightly differently: 'Unless one is born anew,' he told that sincere Pharisee, 'he cannot see the kingdom of God . . . unless one is born of water and the Spirit, he cannot enter the kingdom of God'[35] He was referring to the condition of repentance ('water' representing a baptismal washing from sin), and to the subsequent entry into the believer of God's Spirit. Peter, in his very first sermon after Pentecost, laid down the same condition: 'Repent, and be baptized every one of you in the name of Jesus Christ for the forgiveness of your sins; and you shall receive the gift of the Holy Spirit.'[36]

Throughout the New Testament, as has been amply demonstrated, it is made clear that only those who personally respond to the invitation of Christ are sons of God, members of his kingdom, possessors of his Spirit and sharers in the promises. To argue - as so many advocates of a 'social gospel' have argued - from the proposition that all men, with or without faith, are inheritors of the promises, members of the kingdom of heaven and brothers in Christ, is ludicrously to misrepresent the New Testament. This false assumption, however, obviously leads to the conclusion that the Church must be involved corporately in the social and political life of the world. The world, it is in effect being presupposed, *is* the Church - a view which constitutes a form of apostasy. All men are treated as regenerate, if not sinless, and something near to an ethic of perfection - that ethic which is only appropriate or practical within the context of the community which is actually regenerate - is required from them.

So all kinds of experiments in 'Christian Socialism', imposed by well-intentioned Christian rulers on their peoples, have met with disaster. Stanley Booth-Clibborn refers, for example, to the partly Christian inspiration for the Arusha Declaration in Tanzania under President Nyerere.[37] Certainly, there is no question that the 'Christian Socialist' principles of Trevor Huddleston contributed to Nyerere's attempts to foist collectivist policies upon his people. Yet the experiment, especially the enforced movement of tribes to partake in collective farming, was a failure, economically and socially. As long ago as 1980 the country was forced, as a result of severe food shortages, to face the necessity of agreeing to economic conditions previously rejected as contrary to its socialist principles, and in 1986 President Mwinyi formally declared (following a British-sponsored pilot project on de-villagization) that the Ujama system of collectivization was being abandoned.[38]

Socialist policies adopted by the notably Christian President Kaunda of Zambia, who was influenced by the Christian Socialist thinking of the Methodist missionary leader Colin Morris, were also wholly unsuccessful. Immediately after independence in 1964, Zambia set up hundreds of peasant co-operatives in a bid to increase agricultural production and reduce the country's dependence on commercial farmers. By 1980, only a few of the co-operatives were in existence, while the large state ranches and the ambitious rural reconstruction centre project started in 1975 were scarcely functioning. Now the whole centralized system has collapsed, and President Kaunda, in the first free general election (31 October 1991) since 1968, was rejected by the Zambian people in favour of Mr Chiluba, a believer in private enterprise.[39]

Today, faced as we are with the social and economic failure of socialist experiments immensely larger than those set up in Africa, it might seem unnecessary to point to the error of Christians who have sought to impose collectivist and other principles of 'Christian Socialism' upon society as a whole. But erroneous views die hard, if they die at all. Today we not only have the spectacle of leading church spokesmen continuing to advocate the adoption by governments of such principles - as if they were new and untried ideas - but we have churches and other Christian bodies sanctioning or even actively supporting the use of violence in the interests of egalitarianism and 'more just forms of society'.[40]

One cannot but wonder whether the churches today are not, as a result of their attitude to violence, helping to bring about just such a fearful catastrophe as that created in AD 70 by the attitude of many Jews.

The most important point, however, is not that the political implementation of 'Christian Socialism' has been unsuccessful, tragic though this may sometimes have been, but that the Church's true task, her *mission*, has been compromised and, inevitably, neglected.

St Francis, by a kind of holy intuition, had it right. He was so concerned about following Christ in an apostolic simplicity, returning to the spiritual nature of the Church and spreading her Gospel, that he concluded that the Church in her corporate capacity should not even have possessions, let alone have a secular role, and this ideal, as Chesterton says, 'was in a sense the very reverse of socialist'. What the early Franciscans, invoking the authority of St Francis, 'primarily refused to do', Chesterton points out, 'was what Socialists primarily exist to do; to own legally in their corporate capacity'.[41] In a typically original way, Francis and his followers were making the protest that Luther made three centuries later, that the Church is 'not of this world', so that she is, in the final analysis, invisible.[42] She is truly a 'kingdom of heaven'. Luther, of course, went on to explain, what the Franciscans left unsaid, that the Church exists in this world in the form of her members, and that those members, having both 'heavenly' and 'worldly' roles, have a responsibility to work in and with the world (not just preach to it) by virtue of the latter role.

The single call
The Gospel, the message of the Church, is one that transcends this world and this life altogether. It comprises a new and distinctive revelation about man's

potential in Christ, and, as Kierkegaard would have said, between the actual and the potential for mankind there lies 'an infinite qualitative difference'.

There is only one task for the Church in her corporate capacity - for Christians, that is, as Christians. It is a task quite distinct from that of all other associations of people in this world. If the Church fails in this her appointed task she can be certain that no one else is going to carry it out for her. It is the task which is summed up in that last commission given to her by Christ in person: 'Go therefore and make disciples of all nations, baptizing them in the name of the Father and of the Son and of the Holy Spirit, teaching them to observe all that I have commanded you,' or, in another version, 'Go into all the world and preach the gospel to the whole creation,' or, in a third version, 'Thus it is written, that the Christ should suffer and on the third day rise from the dead, and that repentance and forgiveness of sins should be preached in his name to all nations, beginning from Jerusalem. You are witnesses of these things . . . witnesses in Jerusalem and in all Judea and Samaria and to the end of the earth'.[43]

'The shoemaker to his last', we say. So let the Church remain true to her task, to her single and abiding mission, that of sharing with all men - whatever their race, background, outlook, politics, social or moral standing - a transcendent message of unparalleled hope. As she fulfils this mission she will know that in so doing she is making the greatest of all possible contributions to the material welfare of the world, as demonstrated - to mention but two examples - by the history of the Church in the Roman Empire, and the story of the evangelical revival in England of the eighteenth century.[44] 'Through evangelism,' wrote John Bathgate in 1961, 'lives are radically changed, the Church established, the destiny of men and the character of civilization and the course of history altered.'[45]

We live today in a world which, racked by doubt and disaster, cries out for a hope beyond itself. Let the Church offer to such a world what she alone has it in her power to offer. Let her not, for the living bread, offer a stone.

Notes and References

N.B. For the Gospels Matthew, Mark, Luke and John the abbreviations Mt, Mk, Lk, and Jn are used. Other abbreviations are easily identifiable.

Chapter 1

1. Though not obviously a part of Christian history, about which the first part of this book is concerned, the Jewish War with Rome is relevant to an understanding of the first generation of Christians and their place in society. Indeed, Christian believers were for many years after the death of Jesus considered to be simply another Jewish sect, for Jewish Christians in Judaea tended to go on observing Jewish religious rites whilst Temple worship continued (Acts 2:46, 3:3, 5:42, 21:20-26, 25:8; cf. *also* Acts 18:12-17). The fall of Jerusalem and the destruction of the Temple in AD 70 was significant for the Christian Church, as well as for traditional Judaism; it marked a final break with the old order, and, humanly speaking, it no doubt helped to ensure that Christianity did not remain an alternative form of Judaism rather than become a new and universal religion. Jesus himself clearly considered that the destruction of Jerusalem, which he predicted on several occasions (Mk 13:1, 2; Mt 23:37-24:2; Lk 19:41-44, 21:20-24; *et al.*), was to be significant for his followers, individual Christian believers, as well as for the Jewish nation.

    Some have argued that the Jewish War was in a direct sense a part of Christian history. In *Those Incredible Christians* (London, Hutchinson, 1968), Hugh J. Schonfield argues, p. 100, that 'it was Jewish and Christian Messianism which the Romans were seeking to eradicate', and, p. 107, he concludes: 'The first phase of Christianity was ended by this tragic yet heroic chapter in Jewish history.' His assumption is that the early Jewish believers in Jesus took him as nothing more than a national Messiah. *See* Chapter 2, Note 2, *as also* Chapter 7 of this book.

2. Grayzel, Solomon, *A History of the Jews* (New York, Mentor, 1968 [1947]), p. 102. Cf. Kingdon, H. Paul, 'The Origins of the Zealots', *New Testament Studies*, 19 (October 1972), pp. 74-81, questioning an appendix on 'The Zealots' in Jackson, F.J. Foakes, and Lake, K, *The Beginnings of Christianity* (London, Macmillan, 1920), Vol. I, p. 423. Kingdon's concluding remark, pin-pointing the seminal nature of the Zealot movement for future exponents of violence as a legitimate weapon for religious or ideological expansion, further illustrates the relevance of the study of the Jewish War that follows. He writes: 'It is surely clear that in some sense the term *zēlotēs* stands for a tradition older than Pharisaism or Essenism, which was also, however little Jesus himself may have

been keen on it, to play its part in the later history not only of Islam with its *jihād*, and of Marxism, but also of the Christian Church.' A specific reference by a modern Christian writer to the Jewish War as being responsible for his own support, as a Christian on conscientious grounds, of violent revolutionary movements comes in Colin Morris' book *Unyoung, Uncoloured, Unpoor* (London, Epworth, 1969), p. 122.

Alan Richardson *The Political Christ* (London, SCM, 1973), pp. 43, 44, writes thus of the Zealots, however: 'We must conclude that the New Testament, like Josephus, supplies no evidence for the existence of a political party called Zealots before the outbreak of the Jewish War.' Cf. his Note 3 to Chapter II, where he records that Josephus never refers to the Zealots in his *Antiquities of the Jews*, and that his first reference to the Zealots in his *Wars of the Jews* is when he reaches AD 66, where the term is used of a particular group of militants, not resistance fighters as a whole. Cf. *also* Horsley, R.A., with Hanson, J.S., *Bandits, Prophets, and Messiahs* (Minn., Winston Press, 1985; paperback edition: San Francisco, Harper & Row, 1988), *esp.* the Introduction *and* pp. 190-243, where the argument is similar to that of Richardson.

Of course, Zealotry does not have to have been a coherent movement long before the Jewish War for us to recognize that its antecedents then existed. Cf., further, Note 3, immediately below, *and* Chapter 7, Note 56.

3. Josephus, *War of the Jews*, II, viii, 1; Josephus, *Antiquities of the Jews*, XVIII, i, 1, 4; both translated by Whiston, W. (London, J.M. McGowan [undated]). The terms in which Josephus, in the sections cited from *Antiquities*, describes first Judas, as one 'zealous to draw them [the Jews] to a revolt', and then describes his 'fourth sect of Jewish philosophy', with its 'inviolable attachment to liberty', and acknowledgement of 'God as their only Ruler and Lord', so that 'they also do not value dying any kinds of death, nor . . . heed the deaths of their relations and friends', would seem to suggest that there did exist from AD 6 a coherent party which, whether actually known at the time as the Zealot Party, was something very like a freedom fighting movement. Cf. Lk 6:15 *and* Acts 5:37.

4. Suetonius, *Vespasian*, iv (from his *Lives of the Caesars*).

5. Josephus, *Wars of the Jews*, II, xiv, 3.

6. *Ibid.* II, x, 4.

7. *Ibid.* II, x, v.

8. *Ibid.* II, xii, 1. Cumanus was procurator from AD 48-52.

9. *Ibid.* II, xii, 1-6.

10. *Ibid.* II, xiii, 2-5. Cf. Acts, 21:38.

11. *Ibid.* II, xiii. 6.

12. *Ibid.* II, xvii, 7. The Jewish months are lunar, making the Jewish year one of 354 days. A thirteenth intercalated month occurs every third year. The month of Ab moves between the Gregorian months of July and August.

13. *Ibid.* II, xvii, 2.

14. *Ibid.* V, i, 1, 4.

15. *Ibid.* V, i, 1.

16. *Ibid.* VI, ix, 4.

17. *Ibid.* VI, ix, 3 *and* V, xiii, 7. The month of Tammus moves between June and July.

18. Toynbee, A., *Survey of International Affairs* (London, Royal Institute of International Affairs, 1931), p. 5.

19. Grayzel, *op. cit.*, p. 184.

20. Jn 18:36.

21. Mt 9:13. Cf. Hosea 6:6. It is recorded that when the news of the destruction of the Temple itself was brought to Rabbi Johanan ben Zakkai, and the messenger, a disciple of Johanan, bewailed the loss of the place 'where they make propitiation for the sins of Israel', the master answered: 'My son, let it not grieve thee; we have yet one propitiation equal to it, and what is that but the bestowal of kindnesses? - even as it is written "I desired kindness and not sacrifice."' Cited by Toynbee, A.J., *A Study of History* [abridgement of Volumes 1-6 by D.C. Somervell], (London, Oxford University Press, 1946), p. 435.

Chapter 2

1. Eisler, R., *The Messiah Jesus and John the Baptist* (London, Methuen, 1931); Carmichael, J., *The Death of Jesus* (London, Gollancz, 1963); Brandon, S.G.F., *The Fall of Jerusalem and the Christian Church* (London, S.P.C.K., 1951), and *Jesus and the Zealots* (Manchester University Press, 1967), and *The Trial of Jesus of Nazareth* (London, Batsford, 1968); Schonfield, H.J., *The Passover Plot* (London, Hutchinson, 1965), and *Those Incredible Christians* (London, Hutchinson, 1968), and *The Pentecost Revolution* (London, Macdonald, 1974); Morris, C., *op. cit.*

2. *See* Catchpole, D.R., *The Trial of Jesus: A Study in the Gospels* and *Jewish Historiography from 1770 to the Present Day* (Leiden, E.J. Brill, 1971), pp. 118-26; *also* Chapter 7, *below.*

3. Eusebius, *Eccl. Hist.*, III, v, 2-3; Epiphanius, *Adv. Haer. (Against Heresies)*, xxix, 7; xxx, 2; and *De Mens. et Pond. (On Weights and Measures)*, xv; cited by

Schonfield (1974), pp. 236, 241, in which chapter, entitled 'The Exodus', he also cites (pp. 233-41) Jewish sources to the same effect. Cf. *also* Lietzmann, H., *The Beginnings of the Christian Church*, Vol. I of *History of the Early Church* [translated by B.M. Woolf], (London, The Lutterworth Press, 1949), p. 181.

4. Tertullian, *Apologia*, xxxvii, 2: 'We are but of yesterday, and we have filled your cities, your islands, your station, your boroughs, your council chambers, your very camp, your palace, your senate, your bar; we have left you only your temples.' Cf. Pliny's *Letter to Trajan (The Letters of the Younger Pliny*, London, Penguin Classics, Book X, 96): amongst Christians are 'Roman citizens' and 'individuals of every age and class'.

5. Mt 22:21; Rom. 13:1-7; I Peter 2:13-17; I Tim. 2:1, 2; 6:1, *et al.*

6. Jn 18:36; Lk 17:21; I Corinth. 15:50; Coloss. 1:13, 14. Cf. Ephes. 6:12-17; II Corinth. 10:3, 4.

7. Cf. Westcott, B.F., *The Two Empires* (London, Macmillan, 1909), pp. 55f.

8. Mt 16:21-23; Mk 10:35-37; Lk 18:31-34, 19:11, 22:49. Cf. Acts 1:6.

9. Mt 28:19, 20; Acts 1:6-8. Cf. Fox, R.L., *Pagans and Christians* (London, Viking, 1986; Penguin edition, 1988), p. 299, writing of the early Christians' attitude to slavery: 'Christians aimed to reform the heart, not the social order'.

10. Butterfield, H., *Christianity in European History* [The Riddell Memorial Lectures, 1951], (London, Collins, 1952), p. 11. Cf. Fox, R.L., *op. cit.*, p. 422: 'During their years of persecution, Christians are not known to have attacked their pagan enemies: they shed no innocent blood, except their own . . . never rebelling against the Emperor's temporal rule.' Fox gives a detailed study of the persecution of Christians in the Roman Empire on pp. 419-92 of his work.

11. Butterfield, H., *op. cit.*, p. 11.

12. 'Azzām, 'Abdul Rahmān, *The Eternal Message of Muhammad* (New York, Mentor, 1965 [1964]), p. 171.

13. *Ibid.* p. 171. The sack of Constantinople in 1204 by the fourth Crusade is one example of Christian fighting Christian; the inquisition against the Albigenses is another. *See* Acton, *Lectures on Modern History* (London [Macmillan, 1906], Fontana edition, 1960), p. 113.

14. 'Atīya, 'Azīz, *Crusade, Commerce and Culture* (New York, John Wiley & Sons, Inc., 1966 [1962]), pp. 18, 22, *et al.*

15. Cf. Neill, S., *A History of Christian Missions* (London, Penguin [Pelican Original], 1964), pp. 113-15. He concludes: 'To every Muslim in the Mediterranean lands the Crusades are an event of yesterday, and the wounds are ready

at any moment to break out afresh.' With which comment we may compare an article, 'Bitter legacy of the old crusaders', in *The Daily Telegraph*, 24 February 1991, in which Gerald Butt writes: 'Among many Arabs the current involvement [the Gulf war of January/February, 1991] of the West in the region is stirring unhappy memories and prompting comparisons with foreign adventures from the distant past . . . the crusades.' Cf. also President Bush's remarks in Washington on 27 January 1992, linking his belief in Christ to the US's mission and to the nation's 'success' in the 1991 Gulf war; his remarks were described later in 1992 by Mr M.T. Mehdi - Secretary General of the National Council on Islamic Affairs in New York - as deeply offensive to Muslims and serving to 'confirm the belief in the Muslim world that last year's war on Iraq was another crusade by Christians against Islam'. (See *MECC Newsreport*, April 1992, p. 7).

Others have argued that the fact that the conversion of Muslims was never amongst the motives for the Crusades means that they need not be deplored as a blot upon the Christian missionary movement, to which they never truly belonged; *see* Campbell, J. McLeod, *Christian History in the Making* (London, Church Assembly Press and Publications, 1946), p. 25, who quotes words of Professor Ernest Barker in *The Legacy of Islam*. Such an argument misses the point, however. The Crusades were Church-sponsored, and as such they constituted the grossest betrayal of her true mission.

16. Chesterton, G.K., *St Francis of Assisi* (London, Hodder & Stoughton, paperback edition, 1960 [1923]), p. 153.

17. Mt 10:40.

Chapter 3

1. I Tim. 4:1-5; Coloss. 2:16-23.

2. Lietzmann, H., *The Era of the Church Fathers*, Vol. IV of *History of the Early Church* (London, The Lutterworth Press, 1951), p. 142.

3. Fisher, H.A.L., *A History of Europe* (London, Fontana Library, 1960 [1935]), Vol. I, p. 188.

4. Walbran, J.R. (ed.), *Memorials of Fountains Abbey* (Surtees Society 42, [1863]) i. 15; cited by Southern, R.W., *Western Society and the Church in the Middle Ages* (London, Pelican, 1970), p. 251.

5. Southern, R.W., *op. cit.*, p. 257.

6. A few still believed in evangelism and spiritual conversion. Brother Albert of Mantua, for instance, is recorded by the Chronicles of Bologna to have preached in that city, 'where many were converted', in 1204 - two years before the conversion of St Francis. See *Corpus Chronicorum Bononiensium*, edited by A. Sorbelli, ii. p. 68; cited by Southern, R.W., *op. cit.*, p. 273.

Chapter 4

1. Southern, R.W., *op. cit.*, p. 276.

2. *Ibid.* p. 285. He writes in a note: 'Estimates of numbers in the two Orders differ very widely. For the Franciscans, *see* Moorman, *op. cit.*, 155-76, 351 [Moorman, J., *History of the Franciscan Order*, 1968]; and for the Dominicans, besides Walz [Walz, A., *Compendium Historiae Ordinis Praedicatorum*, 2nd edn, 1948], *see* F. Mandonnet, *Saint Dominique*, 1937, i, 187-8, and (for England) Hinnebusch, *The Early English Friars Preachers*, 1951, pp. 271-8. The earliest official list of Franciscan houses in 1331 is printed in Eubel, *Provinciale Vetustissimum*, 1892.'

3. *Extravagantes Communes*, I, viii, 1 (Friedberg, *Corpus Iuris Canonici*, ii, 1246); cited by Southern, R.W., *op. cit.*, p. 133. The verse quoted from the Bible is Jeremiah 1:10.

4. Southern, R.W., *op. cit.*, p. 143.

5. *Ibid.* p. 143, who refers the reader to see, on this subject, M. Maccarrone, *Vicarius Christi: storia del titola papale (Lateranum, nova series*, xviii, 1952).

6. Kempf, F. (ed.), *Registrum Innocentii III papae super Negotio Romani Imperii (Miscellanea Historiae Pontificiae*, xii, 1947); cited by Southern, R.W., *op. cit.*, p. 144.

7. Poole, R.L. (ed.), *Historia Pontificalis*, 1927, p. 84; cited by Southern, R.W., *op. cit.*, p. 137.

8. Bliss, W.H. *et al.* (eds), *Calendar of Entries in the Papal Registers*, iii, pp. 4-8, 95-181; cited by Southern, R.W., *op. cit.*, p. 138.

9. *De Ecclesia*, edited by J. Loserth (London, 1886), p. 76; cited by Parker, G.H.W., *The Morning Star* (Exeter, Paternoster, 1965).

10. Cf. Boehmer, H., *Der Junge Luther* (Muhlenberg Press, 1946; English translation, *Martin Luther: Road to Reformation*, London, Thames & Hudson, 1957), p. 98.

11. *Ibid.* p. 110, 111.

12. *Open Letter to the Christian Nobility*; preamble on the secular powers. For the full text, see *Works of Martin Luther* (Philadelphia, NJ, Muhlenberg Press, 1959), Vol. 44, pp. 212-15.

13. Boehmer, H., *op. cit.*, p. 415. Boehmer points out that Luther almost certainly did not say the famous words attributed to him: 'Here I stand. I can do no other'.

Chapter 5

1. Boehmer, *op. cit.*, pp. 378-9.

2. For the full text of this tract, see *Works of Martin Luther*, edition as cited, Vol. 46, pp. 49-55.

3. Boehmer, *op. cit.*, p. 378. Luther's view, following St Augustine, was that here on earth there are two 'kingdoms' or 'realms', that of God, or Christ, and that of the world. He believed that the two kingdoms should never be confused, and that therefore the Church should never become political. For a clear summary of his argument *see* Bernard M. Reardon, *Religious Thought in the Reformation* (London, Longman, 1981), pp. 85-7. Cf. *also* Villa-Vicencio, C., *Between Christ and Caesar: Classic and Contemporary Texts on Church and State* (Grand Rapids, Mich. Eerdmans, 1986), pp. 39-43; *and* pp. 49-54, where a part of Luther's tract of 1523 *Secular Authority: To What Extent It Should Be Obeyed*, including his section on 'The Two Kingdoms', is quoted.

   It was in the light of his belief in the two kingdoms that Luther wrote as follows about the peasant's pursuit of their claims: 'The peasants ought rightly let the name of Christian alone and act in some other name, as men who want human and natural rights, not as those who seek Christian rights.' (*See* Luther's *An Admonition to Peace*, as cited by Steven Ozment, *The Age of Reform, 1250-1550* (London, Yale University Press, 1980), p. 241).

4. Chadwick, O., *The Reformation* (London, Penguin, 1964), p. 356.

5. *See* Hill, C., *Intellectual Origins of the English Revolution* (London, Oxford University Press, 1965; Panther Books, 1972).

6. *See* Cragg, G.R., *The Church and the Age of Reason* (London, Penguin, 1960), p. 37f.

7. *Ibid.* p. 129.

8. *Ibid.* p. 142.

9. *Ibid.* p. 143.

Chapter 6

1. *See* Cragg, *op. cit.*, p. 143.

2. *Ibid.* p. 156. Cf. Bready, J. Wesley, *England: Before and After Wesley* (London, Hodder & Stoughton, 1938).

3. *See* Vidler, A.R., *The Church in an Age of Revolution* (London, Penguin, 1961), p. 154, where he mentions that Pope Pius IX was spoken of as 'the vice-God of

humanity', and that one leading French ultramontane referred to him as the continuation of the Incarnate Word.

4. *See* his *Kingdom and Christ* (London, Macmillan, 1842), Vol. II; cited in *The National Church and the Social Order* (London, Church Information Board for the Social and Industrial Council of the Church Assembly, 1956), p. 90.

5. *See* Masterman, N.C., 'The Mental Processes of the Revd F.D. Maurice', in *Theology*, Vol. LXVIII, No. 535, Jan., 1965, pp. 50, 51.

6. Vidler, *op. cit.*, pp. 95, 96.

7. *Ibid.* p. 112, 123-5. Germany remained *par excellence* the provenance of the onslaught on orthodox Christianity, as Kenneth Hamilton points out in *Earthly Good: The Churches and the Betterment of Human Existence* (Grand Rapids, Mich., Eerdmans, 1990), p. 62: 'In the nineteenth century, Germany was the center of all progressive philosophical and theological thought'; and amongst such thinkers was 'the most influential theologian since Schleiermacher, Albrecht Ritschl'. In fact Hamilton considers Ritschl, who 'saw Jesus as a man in line with the Hebrew prophets . . . preaching the kingdom of God, or "the organization of humanity through action inspired by love"', as the real origina-tor of Christian Socialism. Hamilton writes (p. 63): 'Ritschlian theology inspired the Social Gospel movement, with its program of reform through participating in democratic political institutions.' However, the publication of Ritschl's most influential work, *The Christian Doctrine of Justification and Reconciliation* (Germany, 1874; English translation by H.R. Mackintosh and A.B. Macauley, Edinburgh, T & T Clark, 1900) post-dated the contribution of F.D. Maurice and the foundation of the Christian Socialist movement in England.

8. Sherrard, P., 'The Desanctification of Nature', in *Sanctity and Secularity: the Church and the World*, from 'Studies in Church History', ed. Derek Baker, Vol. 10 (Oxford, Blackwell, 1973), p. 10.

9. Vidler, *op. cit.*, p. 121. Cf. Percy Dearmer, writing in the pamphlet *Socialism and Individualism*, 1890, p. 11: 'Christians must be Utopians; nothing is more certain - man is moving to perfection, as scientific discovery proves.' (Available in Bishop Phillpott Library, Truro, No. 261.). Cf. *also* Walter Rauschenbusch's pronouncement, some years later, that the theory of evolution 'has prepared us for understanding the idea of a Reign of God toward which all creation is moving . . . Translate the evolutionary theories into religious faith and you have the doctrine of the Kingdom of God' (*Christianizing the Social Order*, New York, Macmillan, 1912, p. 90; cited by Dorrien, G.J., *Reconstructing the Common Good: Theology and the Social Order*, New York, Orbis, 1990; paperback edition, 1992, p. 25).

10. Westcott, B.F., *Social Aspects of Christianity* (London, Macmillan, 1887), p. 8.

11. *Ibid.* pp. 9, 10.

12. *Ibid.* p. 15.

13. *Ibid.* p. 73.

14. Westcott, B.F., *Lessons from Work* (London, Macmillan, 1901), p. 337. For the Church's efforts today as international peacekeeper, *see* Appendix **(xxvi)**.

15. *Ibid.* p. 333.

16. Cited by Carmichael, J.D., and Goodwin, H.S., *William Temple's Political Legacy* (London, Mowbray, 1963), p. 2.

17. Westcott, B.F. (1887), p. 12.

18. Westcott, B.F. (1901), p. 401.

19. Most notable were the following: Washington Gladden, whose early ministry and writings of the late 1870s have been seen as marking the inception of Christian Socialist thinking in America; Walter Rauschenbusch and the group, including Leighton Williams and Nathaniel Schmidt, which formed around him in 1887; the Episcopalian W.D.P. Bliss. In 1889 Williams and Rauschenbusch launched the Christian Socialist monthly *For the Right*, and in the same year Bliss founded the Society of Christian Socialists, with its periodical, *The Dawn*. Then, in 1893, Rauschenbusch, Williams and Smith formed a Christian Socialist association for Baptists called 'Brotherhood of the Kingdom', opening the membership later to Christians of other denominations. (*See* Dorrien, G.J., *op. cit.* [paperback edition, 1992], pp. 19-24).

20. By 1925, of course, the tide of Christian Socialism was in full flood. As Kenneth Hamilton writes (*op. cit.*, p. 63): ' . . . in the years immediately following World War I, many of the clergy left their pulpits to enter political life - in order to "advance the kingdom".' In particular, the central message of the social gospel, the idea that the Kingdom of God could be built on earth, had received an enormous boost from a book which was to become something of a bible to the movement, Walter Rauschenbusch's *A Theology for the Social Gospel* (New York, Macmillan, 1917; London, 1918). The corner-stone of Rauschenbusch's thinking in this book is summed up by a sentence from an earlier book [*Christianity and the Social Crisis*, New York, Hodder & Stoughton/Macmillan, 1907, p. xiii; cited by Dorrien, G.J., *op. cit.*, p. 28]: 'The essential purpose of Christianity is to transform human society into the Kingdom of God by regenerating all human relations and reconstituting them in accordance with the will of God.'

21. See *Church Times*, 24 & 31 August 1973. What the Orthodox leaders said is worth quoting. Archbishop Athenagorus of Thyateira and Great Britain, who

had represented the Ecumenical Patriarchate of Constantinople on the W.C.C. since 1948, said (in a sermon in Birmingham on 19 August 1973) the following: 'The heart of the W.C.C. has lost its religious pulse and, being overwhelmed by the notions of those who see Christianity as another social movement of history which is not far from economic utilitarianism, tends to equate the "salvation today" as financial assistance and rehabilitation of the underdeveloped, of those who fight against racial discrimination. But the concept of salvation today cannot be different from the concept of salvation yesterday . . . I feel that the Ecumenical Movement on account of the decisions of the W.C.C. has lost its spiritual orientation and lives without a truly Christian heart . . . instead, today it deals with matters that are within the sphere of politics and as such they belong to the United Nations Organization.'

A week later Patriarch Pimen of Moscow and All Russia sent a letter to the Central Committee of the W.C.C. in which he also criticized the Bangkok Conference: 'Nothing,' he wrote, 'is said about the ultimate goal of salvation - in other words, about the eternal life in God. Almost exclusive emphasis on "horizontalism" in the cause of salvation may lead many Christians to whom the sacred traditions of the ancient Church are clear to the opinion that, in the ecumenism of today, there appears a new temptation of being ashamed to preach Christ crucified and resurrected, God's power and wisdom. Due to this temptation and false fear of appearing not quite up to date, the fear to lose popularity, the very essence of his gospel is passed over in silence.'

On the overall stance of the Eastern Orthodox Church today in relation to the world order, *see* Villa-Vicencio, C., *op. cit.*, who cites (p. 182) 'Thy Kingdom Come: the Orthodox Contribution' to the W.C.C. Commission on World Mission and Evangelism, Melbourne, 1980: 'In speaking of poverty the Church does not identify its message with the political and social programmes of our time.' He also cites (p. 182) 'Just Development for Fullness of Life: an Orthodox Approach', submitted to the W.C.C. Commission on the Churches' Participation in Development, Kiev, 1982: 'The way of the Gospel is not . . . the violent overturn or change of existing economic, social or political structures. But the Church is in the world to be a blessing, a light and an inspiration . . . the Church has to offer herself . . . as an example of justice, participation and flowering of life.' (For the full texts of the documents, *see* Villa-Vicencio, pp. 185-94).

22. See *Church Times*, 31 May 1974, reporting an Ascension Day conference by the Confessing Fellowships in the Evangelical Churches in Germany which challenged the W.C.C. to abandon false ecumenism as a socio-political emphasis amounting to a 'falsification of the gospel'. In the same issue there was a report about the furore created in the Canadian Churches by W.C.C. grants to liberation movements.

In the *Church Times*, 28 June 1974, there was reported an attack on the W.C.C. by Canon Albert Dubois, President of the American Church Union, who described the W.C.C. as 'Anti-Christ'. In a Trinity Sunday sermon in Washington, DC, he said that ever since the beginning of the century a false religion had been growing like a cancer; the W.C.C. promoted a false ecumenism - 'that is, false efforts to unify Christians on a humanistic, man-centred programme.' Christ, Canon Dubois said, was no longer the unique gift of God but simply a 'man for others' - one of many teachers God had sent to various cultures, a good example. There was to be a moratorium on seeking to convert, and dialogue was substituted for Christ's great commandment to go, teach, to the ends of the world - dialogue in the hope of creating a new, man-made religion out of bits and pieces of Buddhism, Islam, Mao-ism, Marxist revolutionary and man-centred liberation efforts, and such elements of Christianity as do not give offence. God was relegated to a position like that of a constitutional monarch 'who condescends from time to time to emerge from his remoteness to approve of our efforts to create utopia on earth without the need of any real help from him.'

In June, 1975, the Christian Affirmation Campaign published its first pamphlet in which the writer, Bernard Smith, asserted, quoting W.C.C. official documents, that the W.C.C. believed participation in violent revolution was a Christian duty. (See *Church Times*, 6 June 1975).

23. Westcott, B.F. (1901), p. 436.

24. Cited by Carmichael and Goodwin, *op. cit.*, p. 3.

25. *Ibid*. p. 5.

26. *Ibid*. pp. 11, 12, where the Resolutions of the Malvern Conference are quoted in full.

27. Temple, W., *Christianity and Social Order* (London, Penguin, 1942), p. 75.

28. Cf. the B.C.C. report *The Era of Atomic Power* (1946).

29. Temple, W., *op. cit.*, (London, S.C.M., 1940), p. 25.

30. Cited by Carmichael and Goodwin in 'The Church Political', from 'Sinews of Society', Part III of *Right Turn*, a symposium edited by Dr Rhodes Boyson (London, Churchill Press, 1970), p. 109.
   The incisiveness of Henson's statement contrasts with Bishop Gore's approach: 'Christ alone, in direct quickening grace, can restore the moral health of individuals, but there are preliminary obstacles to its influence to be removed. Bad dwellings, inadequate wages, inadequate education, inability to use leisure - these are stones which lie upon the graves of men spiritually dead. We must take away the stones.' (*See* Gore's pamphlet, *c.* 1894, *The Social Doctrine of the Sermon on the Mount*; cited by Lindsay, A.D., *The Two Moralities: Our Duty to God and to Society*, London, Eyre & Spottiswoode, 1940, p. 87).

31. Cf. his best-selling book, *Naught for Your Comfort* (London, Collins, 1956; Fontana, 1957), p. 184: ' . . . I would defend in any company the right of the Church to take part in the political life of the country . . .'; and on p. 176: 'It always amuses me to hear discussions on the hoary old problem of religion and politics and to think what such discussions would have meant to men like Jeremiah and Amos and Isaiah and Ezekiel. For in fact half their time was spent

in trying to bring home to the men of their day the fact that God was directly concerned in the way society was organized: in the way wealth was distributed: in the way men behaved to one another. In short - politics. It is only in our post-reformation day when religion has become individualistic, that we have created this dichotomy. And thank God the tide has already turned and is running fast in the opposite direction: except in South Africa.' *See also* Chapter 9, Note 24.

32. Cf. especially David Sheppard's *Built as a City* (London, Hodder & Stoughton, 1974), *Bias to the Poor* (London, Hodder & Stoughton, 1983), and (with Derek Worlock), *Better Together* (London, Penguin, 1989). In the first-mentioned Sheppard weaves together history, sociology, theology, and his own experience to make an analysis of inner city problems. The last hundred pages draw out lessons for the Church today, analyse its nature, reappraise its task and outline a 'Gospel' for 'the City'. In *Bias to the Poor* the argument is that, according to Jesus, the materially poor are especially favoured by God and that the wealthy are the enemies of his Kingdom; any other interpretation of, for instance, such statements by Jesus as 'Blessed are you poor' (Luke 6:20, RSV) is wrongly to 'spiritualize' the Gospel (*op. cit.*, pp. 12-14). In *Better Together*, Sheppard and Worlock call the policies of the New Right under Mrs Thatcher un-Christian (*op. cit.*, pp. 290-4). For a critique of Sheppard's argument in *Bias to the Poor* see William Oddie's 'Christian Socialism: An Old Heresy?' in *The Kindness that Kills*, edited by Digby Anderson (London, S.P.C.K., 1984), pp. 123f; and for a further critique of the methods employed by Sheppard and other church writers on sociological themes, *see* Digby Anderson in the same symposium, pp. 157f, 'Eating Sheppard's Pie: Hints on Reading the Sociological Gospel'. *See also* Chapter 9, Note 28, *below*.

33. See *The Times*, 20 April 1991, reporting Dr George Carey's enthronement as Archbishop on 19 April: 'Carey pledges the church to a high political profile', by Ruth Gledhill. In his enthronement sermon, Dr Carey said that the 'earthed gospel takes us directly into the marketplace of the world. No Church can or should avoid political comment when freedom, dignity and worth are threatened. The cross of Jesus Christ . . . places us alongside the oppressed, the dispossessed, the homeless, the poor and the starving millions of our planet.' *See also*, for Dr Carey's condemnation of businessmen, Appendix (**xxv**), (d); *and*, for Dr Carey and world peace, Appendix (**xxvi**).

With regard to 'refutations' of evangelical orthodoxy, *see*, for example, *Christian Faith and Political Hopes: A Reply to E.R. Norman* (London, Epworth Press, 1979), with contributors Charles Elliot, Duncan B. Forrester, Peter Hinchcliff, Daniel Jenkins, David Jenkins, John Kent, James Mark, Robert Moore, Haddon Willmer. They were replying to Edward Norman's 1978 Reith Lectures, published as *Christianity and the World Order* (Oxford University Press 1979). Cf. *also*, responses to two articles, critical of the assumption that the Church should corporately involve herself in the socio-political sphere, published by the present writer. Firstly, 'The Politics of Jesus', published in *Crusade*, May 1974, prompted a reply in the form of a monograph by Christopher Sugden, *Social Gospel or No Gospel?* (Bramcote, Grove Books, 1975). The assumptions in this booklet are similar to those of David Sheppard in *Built as a City* (*see* Note 32, *above*). Secondly, 'A Question of Involvement', published in *New Fire*, Autumn 1976 (Vol. iv, No. 28), called forth a reply in the journal's Winter issue of 1976 (pp. 231, 232) by Giles Ecclestone, Secretary of the Church of England Board for Social Responsibility, in which he strongly rejected the idea that the Church should 'adopt a view of its mission which limited it to the evangelizing of individuals'. He also wrote: 'I wish he [Mr Blair] had given some indication of the significance he attaches to the historical experience of the Church in engaging with the actuality of social and political life.' Hence Part I of this book.

34. *See* Norman, E.R., *op. cit.* (Note 33, *above*, para. 2). As Julia Neuberger has written, reviewing Stewart Lamont's book, *Church and State*, London, Bodley Head, 1989), in *The Sunday Times*, 13 August 1989; it has been 'more or less generally accepted in the late 1980s, that it is no longer possible to talk authoritatively about the division between church and politics.' Cf. *also* David Willey's book *God's Politician: John Paul at the Vatican* (London, Faber, 1992), and its dustcover remarks: 'Catholics and non-Catholics alike cannot help but recognize that, for this Polish Pope, politics and religion are inseparably linked.'

35. Further evidence of the Church's 'politicization' in recent years is given in the Appendix.

36. e.g., the statement by Canon Burgess Carr, General Secretary of the All Africa Conference of Churches, that God has 'sanctified violence into a redemptive instrument for bringing into being a fuller human life.' (*The Struggle Continues*, Official Report, Third Assembly, All Africa Conference of Churches, Nairobi, 1975, p. 78; cited by Edward Norman, *op. cit.*, p. 60; the relevant passage from Canon Carr's address, originally delivered in Lusaka, 14 May 1974, is cited by Villa-Vicencio, *op. cit.*, p. 177). Cf. *also* the Lambeth Conference of Anglican Bishops, 1988, which in its 'Christianity and Social Order' section affirms that 'the overthrow of unjust systems is a gospel imperative', and that it 'understands those who, after exhausting all other ways, choose the way of armed struggle as the only way to justice . . .' *See* Appendix (**xi**), citing a report in *The Daily Telegraph*, 5 August 1988; *see also* Note 37, *immediately below*.

37. 'Liberation theology', as originally proposed, argues that the 'institutionalized violence' of bourgeois society justifies the use of revolutionary violence for political change. Authority for this is claimed from the New Testament, which is expounded in such a way that Jesus is seen as a political liberator. Cf. Gustavo Gutiérrez, *Teologia de la liberación, Perspectivas* (Lima, C.E.P., 1971; English translation published as *A Theology of Liberation: History, Politics and Salvation*, London, S.C.M., 1971), in which *see esp.* pp. 103, 175. Cf. *also* Chapter 1, Note 2, para. 1; *and* Appendix (**iii**) *and* (**xviii**).

In his Hibbert Lecture, 1985, entitled 'The God of Freedom and the Freedom of God', David Jenkins, Bishop of Durham, called for the development of a 'British liberation theology' - that is, a theology concerned with 'renewing faith in God and also in renewing our politics'. It would 'take some of the diagnoses of Marxism very seriously', would 'challenge and confront' the error of 'entrepreneurial individualism', and would seek to build up 'communities of endurance' prepared to face 'uncertainty, turbulence, violence' as they committed themselves to 'fighting through to a way forward'. (*See* Jenkins, D., *God, Politics and the Future*, London, S.C.M., 1988, pp. 113-16; for the whole lecture, *see* pp. 105-116).

38. *See*, for example, the Church Missionary Society Annual Sermon for 1979, quoted in Appendix (**viii**).

39. Contrast Jn 3:17; 12:47; I Corinth. 5:12, 13a. Church leaders and councils may legitimately, of course, guide their own church members on questions of morality, and such questions will sometimes relate to the Christian's proper response to political issues - like the 'civil disobedience' of early Christians who refused to uphold the State religion, or of German Christians under the Nazis who refused to inform on the Jews, or, in more recent times, of South African Christians who refused to support the government in its policy of encouraging racially segregated worship. But this is a far cry from the condemnation by the Church through her leaders or councils of groups who do not have any church affiliation - all too common a habit among Anglican Church leaders in recent years. *See* Appendix (**xxv**) for several examples of such condemnation, implied or explicit.

40. Cf. Lietzmann, H. (1949), p. 15; *also* Bruce, F.F., *The Spreading Flame* (Exeter, Paternoster, 1958), p. 58.

Chapter 7

1. Kahl, J., *Das Elend des Christentums* (Hamburg, 1968; translated into English as *The Misery of Christianity*, London, Penguin, 1971), p. 102.

2. *Ibid*. pp. 103-21.

3. *Ibid*. p. 118.

4. *Ibid*. p. 118.

5. *Ibid*. p. 120.

6. *Ibid*. pp. 120, 121.

7. *Ibid*. p. 103.

8. e.g. C.H. Dodd, *The Founder of Christianity* (London, Collins, 1971), who cites the early second century writers Pliny and Tacitus, and the Jewish Babylonian Talmud, as well as the New Testament, in seeking to shed light on the historical Jesus; Pliny, *Correspondence with Trajan*, letter 96; Tacitus, *Annals* xv, 44;

Babylonian Talmud, *Tractate Sanhedrin*, 43b. Further, Professor J.R. Porter has argued, in a letter to *The Times* (4 April 1991), that Josephus probably mentioned Jesus. Referring to the famous passage about Jesus, the so-called *Testimonium Flavianum*, in the received text of *Antiquities*, 18, Professor Porter points out that, in contrast to the view that it is 'a later and wholly Christian interpolation', there is 'an increasing tendency among scholars rather to see here an original reference to Jesus, which has been edited and expanded by one or more Christian copyists'. In support of his argument, Professor Porter cites an Arabic version of the *Testimonium Flavianum* in a work by a tenth century bishop of Hierapolis, from which all the distinctively Christian references are markedly absent. *See also* Note 12, *below*.

9. Schonfield, H., *The Passover Plot* (London, Hutchinson, 1965). *See* Part I, Chapter 2, Note 1; *see also* p. 240 in the 1985 edition of *The Passover Plot* (Shaftsbury, Element Books): 'When we come to assess the character and worth of the Gospels it is important to know that behind them is a considerable amount of material about Jesus, which fortunately, because of Roman oppression in Palestine between AD 45 and 55, had been conveyed to other lands before the outbreak of the fatal Jewish revolt against Rome . . . Consequently . . . we can be convinced that Jesus really lived and that a good deal reported about him is worthy of credence . . .'

10. *The Empty Tomb* (London, Panther, 1963), p. 18. Cf, *also* the modern school of scholars who set great store by what they call the 'legitimating' by the early Christian community (especially a 'Johannine Community', which included Jews thrown out of the synagogue after AD 70) of its existence by working over the first traditions about Jesus to make him into the incarnate God who died and rose from the dead. This is the stance of Maurice Casey, in *From Jewish Prophet to Gentile God* (Cambridge, James Clarke, 1991), *see* pp. 38, 97-120, 153, 156-9, who writes of the resurrection, for instance (pp. 105, 107): 'The story of the empty tomb is secondary. It performs the same legitimating role as in all resurrection narratives of any length . . . It originated among disciples who knew resurrection as the normative form of survival after death.'

Both Furneaux and Casey, however, affirm a substantial authenticity for their source materials. Furneaux writes (p. 143): 'One thing seems certain, Jesus must have said most or many of the words attributed to him. Whatever else is doubtful, his basic teaching remains.' Casey, believing that the gospels were written '30 odd years' after Jesus' death, tells us (p. 57) that he has 'assumed that both Mark and Q [the supposed common source behind Matthew and Luke] contain a large quantity of authentic source material, much of which was written down in Aramaic by Jews long before the writing of the Gospels'. *See further*, Note 12, *below*.

11. e.g. Morison, F., *Who Moved the Stone* (London, Faber, 1930); Perry, M.C., *The Easter Enigma* (London, Faber, 1959), *esp*. pp. 90-119; Ramsay, A.M., *The Resurrection of Christ* (London, Bles, 1945). Cf. *also* Dodd, C.H., *op. cit.*, pp. 163f; and the beginning of Chapter 8 of this book.

12. For an early date for all four gospels see Robinson, J.A.T., *Redating the New Testament* (London, S.C.M., 1976). Cf. Wenham, J.W., *Redating Matthew, Mark and Luke* (London, Hodder & Stoughton, 1991); *also* Thiede, C., *Jesus: Life or Legend* (Oxford, Lion, 1990); Bruce, F.F., *Are the New Testament Documents Reliable?* (London, I.V.F., 1943); Mascall, E.L., *The Secularisation of Christianity* (London, Darton, Longman & Todd, 1965), pp. 213-82 ('Fact and the Gospels'); Dodd, C.H., *op. cit.*, pp. 163f.

The second century writer, Papias of Hierapolis, tells us that 'Matthew compiled the Logia in the "Hebrew" tongue [i.e. Aramaic], and every one translated them as best he could.' (Eusebius, *Eccl. Hist.*, iii, 39). Thus Matthew, the tax-collector, one of the inner group of Jesus' disciples, probably originally wrote large parts of the gospel that bears his name, if not the whole of it. And Papias also tells us that Mark was using the recollections of the apostle Peter (*Frag.* 2, 15; also recorded in Eusebius, *Eccl. Hist.*, iii, 39). The author of Luke's gospel and the Acts of the Apostles claims to be giving 'a connected narrative' and 'authentic knowledge' about the events described, basing his account, as had others, on the testimony of 'original eyewitnesses'. C.H. Dodd (*op. cit.*, p. 18) concludes: 'It seems fair to assume that he writes in good faith . . . We may take it then that that he was acquainted with a tradition handed down from eyewitnesses and of written narratives based upon it.' The author of John's gospel claims to be the beloved disciple (John 21:23, 24), especially close to Jesus, and Robinson (*op. cit.*, p. 303) states that 'the evidence points strongly to the apostle John'. Later (pp. 309-11) he sums up some of the difficulties in postulating anyone other than such an eyewitness as the author. He inclines to a date before AD 70 for the composition of John, as for the composition of almost all the rest of the New Testament.

13. Mt 4:1-11; Mk 1:12, 13; Lk 4:1-13.

14. Cf. parables like the prodigal son, or the good Samaritan. Dodd, *op. cit.*, p. 124, writes: 'The account of the "testing" could no doubt have been compiled retrospectively . . . But we have good reason to believe that Jesus had in fact faced his test and made his decision before even he came out in public . . . It is not at all incredible that he himself depicted the conflict and its issue in some such dramatic and symbolic form.' Richardson, *op. cit.*, p. 45, calls the account of the temptations a 'parable'.

15. Mt 4:4.

16. Mt 4:5-7.

17. Mt 4:8-10.

18. Dodd, *op. cit.*, p. 123.

19. *Ibid*. p. 123.

20. Mt 4:10.

21. See all the gospels, *passim*. For the feedings of the multitudes, *see* Mk 6:35-44 *and* 8:1-9. Other specific examples: for healings and the casting out of demons, *see* Mt 4:23, 24; 8:14-16; 14:34-36; Lk 4:33-41; 5:12-16; 6:17-19; for the declaration of forgiveness, *see* Mt 9:1-8; Lk 5:18-25; for raising the dead, *see* Mt 9:18, 23-26; Lk 7:11-16, Jn 11:1-44.

22. The fact that Jesus usually seemed to wait for people to take the initiative in coming to him for healing demonstrates both a selective approach and a requirement for some prior faith. Other of Jesus' attitudes and actions show further how he believed it necessary in general to limit the scope of his ministry (*see* Mt 10:5-8a; 15:21-28; Jn 5:2-9). As to his miraculous works being signs of some deeper truth, *see*, for example: on the feedings of the multitudes, Mt 16:5-12; Mk 8:14-21; Jn 6:25-51; on his healings, etc, pointing to his true identity and role for those who had eyes to see, Lk 7:19-23; 11:20; Jn 10:25, 37, 38; on bodily healing being the outward sign of sins forgiven, Mt 9:1-8; Mk 2:1-12; on the significance of the healing of a blind man, Jn 9:1-7, 35-41; on the significance of raising Lazarus from the dead, Jn 11:4, 23-27, 40-42. For the fact that signs were not given to those with no prior faith, *see* Mt 16:1-4; Mk 6:1-6; cf. *also* Mt 17:14-20; Mk 9:20-27.

23. Jn 6:1-14.

24. Jn 6:14, 15.

25. Mk 6:45.

26. Dodd, C.H., *op. cit.*, p. 134.

27. Lk 17:20, 21. I give the 'alternative' translation of the Greek *entos* (see *The Greek New Testament*, 3rd edn [corrected], United Bible Societies, 1988). The translation 'within' is the normal meaning of the word (*see* Liddell and Scott, *A Greek-English Lexicon*). The translation 'in the midst of' is possible; if adopted it would presumably mean that Jesus was referring to the kingdom's embodiment, at the moment of speaking, in himself.

28. Except in a future age, after some climactic and catastrophic event. Jesus, on one occasion, describes this new age as 'the new world' or 'regeneration' (Mt 19:28).

29. Mt 5-7; cf. Lk 6:20-49.

30. Mt 13; cf. Mk 4:2-34; Lk 8:4-15.

31. Mt 13:40-43, 49-50.

32. Mt 10:28; Lk 12:4.

33. Mt 10:39; Mk 8:35; Lk 9:24.

34. Jn 12:24, 25.

35. Mt 18:1-4; cf. Mt 19:13-15; Mk 9:36, 37; 10:13-16; Lk 9:46-48; 18:15-17.

36. e.g., on his claim to be Son of God, Mt 11:25-27; 26:63-65; Jn 5:17-18; 10:22-39; as lord of the sabbath, Mt 12:1-13; as exercising power over nature, Mt 8:23-27; Jn 2:1-11; as having the right to forgive sins, Mt 9:1-8; cf. Jn 5:5-9, 14; as having the right to judge, Mt 11:20-24; 16:27; 23:13-39; Jn 5:22-27; 8:16; 9:39; as having authority over the powers of evil, Lk 4:33-36; 9:1; 10:17-20; Jn 12:31; as Messiah, and thus as Son of God, Mt 16:13-20; 26:63-65; Jn 4:25, 26; 10:22-39; 11:25-27.

37. Mt 11:29.

38. Mt 16:21; cf. Mk 8:31; Lk 9:22; Mt 17:12; 20:17-19, 22, 28; Mk 10:45.

39. Mt 21:37, 38, in the parable of the wicked husbandmen. Cf. Mk 12:6-8 *and* Lk 20:13-15.

40. Mt 21:42; Mk 12:10; Lk 20:17; Psalm 118:22.

41. Jn 18:36. Cf. Mt 26:52-54.

42. *See* Liddell and Scott, *op. cit.*, under *basileia*.

43. Jn 18:36. Cf. Mt 26:52-54.

44. Catchpole, D.R., *The Trial of Jesus: A Study in the Gospels and Jewish Historiography from 1770 to the Present Day* (Leiden, E.J. Brill, 1971).

45. *Ibid.* pp. 115, 116.

46. Cf. Schonfield (1965), p. 121. Schonfield describes Jesus' final entry into Jerusalem, then continues: 'The die was cast, and now there could be no turning back. Jesus had boldly and publicly committed himself in the way he had planned. He had accepted the plaudits of the Jewish multitude, chiefly his own Galileans, at the capital of their nation as their rightful ruler. By so doing he had made himself guilty of treason against Caesar. There can be no question about this. The action of Jesus had been intentional and deliberate, and he was fully aware that there could be only one outcome, his arrest and execution. He had contrived, without any show of force and in the most peaceful manner, to make a telling demonstration that he claimed to be the Messiah, forcing the Jewish governmental representatives into a position where they must proceed against him both in the interest of self-preservation and in duty to the Roman emperor, and to do so with the knowledge that he had identified himself to them as the heaven-sent king of Israel.'

47. Catchpole (*op. cit.*, p. 116) quotes from the Jewish writer Paul Winter, *On the Trial of Jesus* (Berlin, de Gruyter, 1961), p. 135: 'Rather than the content of his teaching it was the effect which his teaching had on certain sections of the populace that induced the authorities to take action against him.'

48. Winter, *op. cit.*, pp. 138f.

49. *Ibid.* pp. 148f.

50. Catchpole, D.R., *op. cit.*, pp. 117, 118. The work by Eisler referred to is *The Messiah Jesus and John the Baptist* (London, Methuen, 1931); that by Carmichael is *The Death of Jesus* (London, Gollancz, 1966).

51. Brandon, S.G.F., *Jesus and the Zealots* (Manchester University Press, 1967).

52. Catchpole, D.R., *op. cit.*, p. 120.

53. *Ibid.* p. 120.

54. For such aspirations *see* Mt 20:21; Mk 10:37; Lk 24:27; Jn 6:15; Acts 1:6. Sayings of Jesus are sometimes cited to support the view that Jesus was a political revolutionary of some kind; for example, the saying 'I have not come to bring peace but a sword' (Mt 10:34-39; cf. Lk 12:51, 52a), and his saying about the kingdom of heaven suffering violence and 'men of violence' taking it by force (Mt 11:12; cf. Lk 16:16). Alan Richardson points out (*op. cit.*, p. 46) that in the case of these and other such sayings 'alternative interpretations are more probable'. As regards the two we mention, for example, the former in its context clearly refers to the division sometimes created in a family when a member accepts Jesus, as indicated by Luke's use of the Greek word *diamerismos* = division, where Matthew uses *machaira* = sword; and the latter (somewhat obscure, in any case) is very probably referring, in the word translated 'men of violence' in the RSV (Greek *biastai*, 'violent ones'), to 'the supernatural powers of evil with which the inbreaking reign of God had joined in deadly combat at the coming of Jesus' (cf. Mt 12:24-29; Lk 11:15-22). Richardson also points out (pp. 46, 47) that if such texts appeared to support the view that Jesus commended violent action they would have to be countered by 'the great weight of his teaching about loving one's enemies, doing good to those who hate us ... turning the other cheek, meekness, service of one's fellows, peace-makers ...', etc.

55. Catchpole, D.R., *op. cit.*, p. 122, where he cites Mt 11:12; 12:28, and Lk 17:20, 21 as examples of the kingdom's present realization.

56. But cf. Richardson, *op. cit.*, pp. 41-44, who argues that the epithet 'zealot' (*zēlotēs*, an ordinary Greek word) applied to the disciple Simon does not necessarily indicate that he was anything more than zealous for the Law (cf. Acts 21:20).

57. Catchpole, D.R., *op. cit.*, p. 122.

58. Jn 6:15; see this Chapter, *above*.

59. Mk 12:17; Mt 22:21; Lk 20:25. Cf. Mt 17:25-27, *and* Catchpole, *op. cit.*, pp. 123, 124.

60. Mt 21:12, 13; Mk 11:15-17; Lk 19:45, 46. Cf. Dodd, *op. cit.*, p. 145; 'It was not intended as a *coup d'état*, for he took no steps to follow it up. It must have been something in the nature of a manifesto in action . . . we may note that the very fact that the temple was chosen as the stage for this demonstration made it clear at once that his aims, though he had been acclaimed as a king, were not political; it was the worship of God, not the independence of the Jewish state, that he was concerned with. "Do not turn my Father's house into a market." With these words, according to John, he expelled the traders, according to the elementary principle that the worship of God and the pursuit of gain - and even of funds for religious purposes - are two things and not one. "You cannot serve God and Money" as he had observed earlier.'

61. Catchpole, D.R., *op. cit.*, p. 126.

62. We can leave aside the suggestion that Jesus made no messianic claim - a position which cannot be maintained if only a modicum of credibility is allowed to the gospel records.

63. Cf. Lk 24:25-27 *and* Acts 1:6.

64. Jn 6:15, *etc.*

65. Jn 18:38; 19:4; cf. Mt 27:24; Mk 15:14; Lk 23:4, 14, 20-22.

66. Mt 27:24.

67. Mt 27:24; Mk 15:15.

68. Jn 19:12-16.

69. Schonfield (1965), pp. 149, 150.

70. *Ibid.* p. 150.

71. *Ibid.* p. 150. Schonfield argues (pp. 148, 149) that Jesus was truly guilty of sedition, so that it was not just because of a religious 'blasphemy' that the Jewish Council handed Jesus over to Pilate (cf. Note 46, *above*).

72. *See* Chapter 8, Note 7, paragraph 2.

73. Catchpole, D.R., *op. cit.*, p. 271. Cf. Frank Morison, *op. cit.*, pp. 24-9. Morison's whole reconstruction of the events of the last days of Jesus' life, and its immediate aftermath, has, for a combination of readability and reasonableness, perhaps never been bettered.

Chapter 8

1. Mt 28:19, 20a; cf. Mk 16:15.

2. e.g. David Jenkins, Bishop of Durham, who has said that Christ's resurrection appearances were 'not as literal as all that', suggesting that the disciples' encounters with the risen Jesus had been 'a mixture of vision, conviction and power' (see *Church Times*, 5 May 1989); and, in an interview with Clive Calver, that he thinks the body of Christ could still be rediscovered in a Middle Eastern tomb, but he is not absolutely certain; 'I think the more I am involved in this, the less likely I think that anything that might be called physical reconstruction or resurrection took place.' (See *The Times*, 28 March 1992).

   Bishop Jenkins describes himself as 'fundamentally orthodox' because he believes 'God is incarnate in Jesus', but he qualifies this: 'Possessing a real and true sense that God is incarnate in Jesus and believing in the literal truth of the empty tomb and the virgin birth are not the same thing.' (Interview with Walter Ellis, *The Sunday Telegraph*, 28 June 1987).

3. Implied by Celsus, writing against Christianity in the second century AD revived by the German writers Karl Bahrdt, Karl Venturini and H.E.G. Paulus in the late eighteenth and early nineteenth centuries; taken up by Samuel Butler in 1865. For modern writers, *see* D.H. Lawrence's *The Man Who Died*, the novel by George Moore, *The Brook Kerith* (London, Penguin, 1952). Cf. *also* Hugh Schonfield (1965; *see* Note 7, *below*), *and* Barbara Thiering *Jesus the Man* (London, Doubleday, 1992), both of whom argue that Jesus lost consciousness on the cross after having been drugged, later to revive. For a critical examination of the theory, *see* Perry, M.C., *op. cit.*, pp. 82-9.

4. Furneaux, *op. cit.*, p. 145 (*see* Chapter 7, Note 10, *above*).

5. Mt 28:11-15. Cf. Schonfield (1965), p. 175, and A.N. Wilson *Jesus* (London, Sinclair-Stevenson, 1992). Few have seriously suggested that the Jewish or Roman authorities removed Jesus' body from the tomb. As Frank Morison writes, *op. cit.*, p. 95: 'It is the complete failure of anyone to produce the remains, or to point to any tomb, official or otherwise, in which they were said to lie, which ultimately destroys every theory based upon the human removal of the body.'

   Morison's point also, let it be said, makes it very difficult to accept the theory that belief in Jesus' resurrection was founded on a mistake of the women - that they, and perhaps other disciples later, went to the wrong tomb.

6. Cf. the account of Jesus' resurrection appearance to Thomas in Jn 20:26-29.

7. Mt 28:6; Mk 16:6; Lk 24:2; Jn 20:1-8 (*esp.* v. 8). Further, it is clear that in Peter's preaching (Acts 2:31, 32) the fact that Jesus' body had not seen corruption was significant. As to Paul, it is difficult to see why he should expressly have mentioned that Jesus 'was buried' (I Corinth. 15:4) if it was not his assumption that when Jesus was 'raised on the third day' this involved the transformation of his dead body, leaving the tomb empty. I Corinth. 15:51, 52 fits in with this, too, since the teaching here is that the bodies of all Christians are 'changed', not just left behind, when Christ returns. Cf. *also* Rom. 8:11, 23; Phil. 3:21.

Amongst modern non-Christian writers, Schonfield (*op. cit.*, 1985 edn), p. 180, writes: 'The planning of Jesus for his expected recovery created the mystery of the empty tomb. Without that plan it is difficult to find a valid reason why his body should have been removed from its final resting place, and *without the empty tomb belief in his resurrection would probably not have registered.*' [italics by the present writer]. Schonfield's theory is that Joseph of Arimathea and one or two others had collaborated in a plot to make it appear that Jesus had died on the cross, then been raised from the dead. The plan had worked to the extent that Jesus had not died on the cross, but, aided by a drug, had only lost consciousness. However, after removal from Joseph's bomb Jesus had - though temporarily recovering consciousness - finally succumbed. He was therefore buried elsewhere by the plotters, one of whom was later mistaken for the risen Jesus by most of the disciples (*op. cit.*, pp. 175-9). Cf. *also* Sheehan, T., *The First Coming* (New York, Random House, 1986), who on p. 98 (Vintage Books edition) somewhat coyly admits that Jesus' tomb 'was probably found empty after his death', then proceeds to build his entire thesis on the assumption that it was empty. Mr Sheehan sums up his thesis thus (pp. 171-3): 'One last look, then, at the empty tomb - the real tomb of history . . . In a symbolic sense, the empty tomb was the last word that Jesus the prophet uttered . . . at the end of his mission he, so to speak, dissolved even himself, wiped out every trace, left not even a corpse, only an absolute absence.' Our duty today, he concludes (p. 226), is that of 'recovering the kingdom "without Christ" '. Cf., for Christian writers, Chapter 7, Note 11, *above*.

8. The argument is expanded by C.S. Lewis in *Mere Christianity* (London, Collins, 1952; Fontana, 1955, pp. 51-3).

9. Lk 24:49; Acts 1:8.

10. Acts 2:1-4. Even Schonfield finds it necessary to take the events of that day literally in order to help account for the extraordinary advance of the Church thereafter. In *The Pentecost Revolution* (1974), pp. 110, 111, he writes: 'The indications are that the phenomenon was that of *khamsin*, the sirocco . . . The storm released the overcharged feelings of the disciples . . . they became ecstatic . . . drunk . . . with the wonder of it all, with the glory of it all.'

11. Jn 14:16, 17.

12. Acts 2:22-36.

13. Acts 2:41, 47.

14. Acts 2:47; 5:14; 6:7.

15. Jn 14:18, 20, 23.

16. Jn 15:5.

17. Jn 21:17. Of course, man's love is always a response to God's love for him. It is God who takes the initiative (*see* I Jn 4:19).

18. Lk 15:21.

19. Jn 14:11.

20. Jn 6:28-30, 35, 40.

21. e.g. Mt 8:22; 9:9; Jn 1:43; 21:19, *et al.*

22. *See* Liddell and Scott, *op. cit.*, under *ekalleō*.

23. Mt 16:18 *and* 18:17.

24. Acts 15:14.

25. e.g. Acts 2:40, 47; 4:12; Rom. 10:10; Ephes. 1:13; Hebr. 2:3, *et al.*

26. Jn 15:19.

27. Jn 17:15, 16.

28. *See* Part II, Chapter 7, section 2, *above.*

29. Mt 8:29. Their appeal would appear to be based on the premise that they had some kind of right to exist in the world for the time being.

30. Jn 14:30.

31. Cf. Robinson, *op. cit.*, pp. 285-92.

32. I Jn 5:19.

33. Rom. 8:9-11.

34. I Corinth. 12:27; Coloss. 1:18, *et al.*

35. Coloss. 2:19.

36. Acts 1:3. Cf. I Corinth. 15:3-8.

37. Coloss. 3:1-4.

38. Hebr. 11:1.

39. Hebr. 11:13, 16.

40. Mt 9:15.

41. Mt 25:1-12.

42. Jn 3:28, 29.

43. Ephes. 5:23, 24, 31, 32; II Corinth. 11:2.

44. Ephes. 5:25, 27; cf. II Corinth. 11:2.

45. Rev. 19:7, 8.

46. Rev. 22:17.

47. I Thess. 4:16-18.

48. I Corinth. 15:51, 52a.

49. Coloss. 3:4.

50. Jn 14:1-3.

51. Mt 25:6.

52. Mt 24:42.

53. See *Church Times*, 5 May 1989.

54. Mt 28:19, 20. Cf. Mk 16:15; Lk 24:46-48; Acts 1:8.

Chapter 9

1. Acts 2:44, 45; 4:32-37.

2. Acts 5:4.

3. Mt 18:15-17.

4. I Corinth. 5:1-5, 11-13. Cf. II Thess. 3:14, 15.

5. Mt 5:25, 26, 40.

6. I Corinth, 6:1, 5-7.

7. Mt 5:39. Cf. I Peter 3:9.

8. Mt 5:48.

9. Cf. I Peter 2:19-23.

10. *See* Part I, Chapter 5, paragraph 3.

11. Extracted from Ephes. 6:12-17.

12. Ephes. 6:18.

13. Mk 12:17; Mt 22:21; Lk 20:25.

14. For the references respectively: II Thess. 3:10-12; Rom. 13:6, 7 (cf. Mt 17:24-27); I Peter 2:13-17 *and* Rom. 13:1-5.

15. *Baptist Times*, 13 January 1989.

16. St Paul, in Romans 2:14-16, presupposes a perception of the law of God by men who have received no special revelation. Their perception is instinctive, or natural; theirs is, in fact, a 'natural morality'. Cf. *also* Rom. 1:19-21, referring to man's instinctive, or natural, knowledge of God as one who should be honoured.

17. Cf. Lindsay, A.D., *op. cit.*, *esp.* pp. 1-9.

18. Richardson, A., *op. cit.*, p. 71.

19. Cf. St Augustine's words: 'Faced with the facts of attacks upon the innocent, the command not to kill must give way to the command of love, interpreted as the obligation to protect the innocent.' Cited by Dorrien, G.J., *op. cit.*, p. 95.

20. See *His Strength to Love* (London, Collins/Fontana, 1969 [Hodder & Stoughton, 1964]). The book, a collection of sermons, constitutes the moving testament of one who sought to live in the two realms with absolute integrity. It is not systematic theology, and begs some questions, especially on the validity of 'Christian Socialism' (*see* Fontana edition, pp. 150-5), but his cry is always from the heart.

21. 'Doctrines Which Drive One to Politics', in *Christian Faith and Political Hopes: A Reply to E.R. Norman* (London, Epworth, 1979), p. 143. On p. 144 he expands on this notion: 'An essential (although not sufficient) part of any knowledge of

or belief in the God who is witnessed to by the biblical narratives and declarations is encounters with Him in and through our own "todays". This is of the essence of the prophetic tradition, which is not "biblical" but contemporary in its formation and power.' (*See*, further, on the relevance of the 'prophetic tradition', Note 22, *immediately below*). Cf. Giles Ecclestone, writing as Secretary of the Church of England Board for Social Responsibility, in *New Fire*, Winter 1976, p. 231, in reply to the author's 'A Question of Involvement', *New Fire*, Autumn 1976, pp. 162-6. Ecclestone writes: 'Is it adequate to see in the New Testament ... a guide sufficient for all time to our understanding of what the Church is called to do and be? The single commission to evangelize might be all that was needed when the end of all things was expected any day; it needed to be supplemented, and was supplemented, by a developed view of the Church's place in society, when once the promised end was seen to belong to a different time scale altogether [*sic*]. This can of course be interpreted as mere accommodation to circumstances; it seems to me, rather, an example of the way the Church is kept responsive to genuinely new situations by its Lord.'

22. Contributing to the pamphlet *Socialism and Individualism*, (1890), p. 6 [available for reference in the Bishop Phillpott Library, Truro, File No. 261].

    Westcott here appeals to the Old Testament. 'the Law and the Prophets', as well as to the New, in seeking validation for his political interpretation of Christianity. This is a common expedient of those who preach a 'social gospel'; e.g. T. Huddleston, *op. cit.*, p. 176 (*see* Part I, Chapter 6, Note 31); D. Jenkins, *op. cit.*, pp. 144 (*see* Note 21, *above*), 152; D. Sheppard, who, in a debate with John Pridmore (*Crusade*, March 1975, p. 24) asserted: 'The Kingdom of God isn't a Western idea at all. If you want to understand what Jesus meant you must go straight back into the Old Testament and do some very deep mining' (*see also*, for Sheppard's view, Note 28, *below*, para. 2); C. Sugden, *op. cit.*, p. 9-11, 23; The Kairos Theolgians, *op. cit.* (*see* Appendix (**x**)).

    To claim the authority of the Old Testament in seeking to define the role of the Church, an outpost in the world of God's 'kingdom of heaven', is inappropriate. The New Testament presupposes the validity of the Old Testament for its time, as well as many of the unchanging truths which it affirms. But the Church is not a Church-State, a form of theocracy, as was ancient Israel, for which the historical, legal and prophetic books of the Old Testament came into being. The Church, as such, is not in view in the Old Testament (*pace* the page headings in some old Bible versions). She is, on the contrary, the mystery which Christ came to reveal, and the New Testament expounds. (*See* Mt 13:11; Rom. 16:25-27; Ephes. 3:3-6, 9, 10; 5:32; 6:19; Coloss. 1:24-27).

23. *Hope for the New World* (London, S.C.M., 1940), p. 25.

24. *See* Trevor Huddleston, *op. cit.*, pp. 169, 182, 186. On p. 186 he calls apartheid 'a denial of the very foundation of the Gospel'. The foundation of the Gospel is most truly the forgiveness and new life won for sinful man by Christ, rather than the love of neighbour, which Huddleston suggests. However, apartheid is certainly incompatible with the life of the Church, Christianity in action, since

it obstructs the expression of Christian brotherhood (cf. DeGrucy, J., and Villa-Vicencio, C. (eds.), *Apartheid is a Heresy* (Cambridge, The Lutterworth Press, 1983). It is also a great social evil; but this is not because it is un-Christian but because it is inhuman, unnatural.

For David Sheppard's stance, as illustrated in several publications, *see* Chapter 6, Note 32, *above*, and Note 28 to this Chapter, *below*.

25. The sermon as published by the C.M.S. under the title *The End of the Monopoly Game: Christ's call to the Family of Man* (London, 1973), pp. 2, 3, 5, 10-12.

26. Barth, Karl, 'The Christian Community and the Civil Community', in *Against the Stream* (London, S.C.M., 1954).

27. Temple, *op. cit.*, (London, Penguin, 1942); republished by S.P.C.K., 1976.

28. Sheppard, *op. cit.*, (London, Hodder & Stoughton, 1974). Bishop Sheppard begins the book by affirming that the Christian gospel brings hope to those enslaved by urbanization. It appears to be a material, not spiritual, hope that he is referring to , as witnessed, for instance, by what he says in his chapter entitled 'Power and Powerlessness'; he writes (p. 189): 'Access to good education and participation in the way decisions are made at work must be part of the good news we announce to the poor'. Or again, in the chapter on 'Priority Areas', writing on the question of schools (p. 150): 'The demand of Christian obedience seems to me to give the priority to those children who are most disadvantaged . . . If we have the faith to demonstrate in our schools that we are called to be members one of another, we may find fuller life for the well-established schools rather than their destruction. And we may give richer life to the majority'. The implication in the first passage is that 'good education' and decision sharing are a part of Christ's Gospel, part of the 'good news . . . to the poor' (cf. Lk 4:18); in the second we see an application of the ethical standards of the kingdom of heaven, of perfection, to non-Christian society. It is, in fact, only Christians who (by faith in Christ) are 'members one of another'. Such Christians may long for this brotherhood of 'faith' to be achieved in society at large, but faith has to come first; until men have it, or the great majority have it, society has to order itself on the assumption that men are not 'members one of another' in the sense of possessing mutual brotherly love and a consequent overriding desire to co-operate rather than compete.

Bishop Sheppard is ambivalent, however, on this matter of applying the Church's ethical norms to society as a whole. He has said: 'I don't believe there is a "Christian line" about education, industry, housing and so on' (*Crusade*, March 1975, p. 23), to some extent rescinding his argument in *Built as a City*. On the other hand, much more recently, in his *Better Together* (with Derek Worlock), London, Penguin, 1989, we read, with reference to the policies of Thatcherism (p. 294): 'Looking after Number One . . . cannot be advanced as Christian social justice.' And in the same work, quoting the Church of England report *Faith in the City* (London, Church House Publishing, 1985), para. 3, 13, he writes (p. 292): '"The creation of wealth must go hand in hand with just distribution . . . There is a long Christian tradition reaching back into the Old Testament prophets, and supported by influential schools of economic and political thought, which firmly rejects the amassing of wealth unless it is justly obtained and fairly distributed" . . . These last months have shown the extent to which this basis Christian assumption is rejected by the New Right . . .'.

29. Mt 24:12; Lk 21; 25, 26.

30. Ephes. 1:13.

31. Extracted from Galat. 3:22 to 4:6.

32. Ephes. 6:12.

33. Ephes. 2:1-3.

34. Coloss. 1:4, 13, 14.

35. Jn 3:3, 5.

36. Acts 2:38.

37. *Op. cit.*, p. 12. Cf. Joseph Sipendi, *The Arusha Declaration and Christian Socialism* (Dar es Salaam, 1969), p. 30.

38. See *The Guardian* (Weekly), 30 March 1980: 'Tanzania faces food shortages', by Martha Honey; also *Oman Daily Observer*, 8 December 1990: 'Tanzania in a hurry to ditch home-grown socialism', by Buchizya Mseteka. Mseteka writes: 'President Ali Hassan Mwinyi . . . is moving Tanzania into a new phase of political and economic reform designed to speed up recovery after two decades of stagnation. Analysts and diplomats say Mwinyi's second and last five-year term will see the final ditching of the home-grown brand of socialism associated with the country's first president Julius Nyerere. Critics accuse Nyerere of creating a doctrinaire socialist system which stifled enterprise, stimulated corruption and led to giant-sized bureaucratic inefficiency. With its economy in shambles, Tanzania was dubbed "the sick child of Africa".'

39. See *The Guardian* (Weekly), 30 March 1980: 'Failure of Zambian socialism exposed', by John Borrell; also *The Daily Telegraph* 18 October 1991: 'A Place that's come to bits', in which Fred Bridgland analyses the 'Zambian post-independence story', which he describes as 'one of mammoth incompetence and disaster', concluding that Kenneth Kaunda has 'comprehensively impoverished' the Zambian peasantry ' in 27 years of rule by error'; also *The Sunday Times*, 3 November 1991, where the article by Mike Hall, 'Jubilation for Zambian victor', reports the massive electoral defeat of President Kaunda on 31 October 1991, in favour of Mr Frederick Chiluba, who 'has made a commitment to promote private enterprise and is likely to embark on a rapid programme of privatization'.

With both Tanzania and Zambia we may contrast Botswana, where the regime since independence in 1966 has, while remaining humane, consistently eschewed doctrinaire socialism, with the results highlighted in 'Focus: Botswana', *The Times*, 30 September 1991, which 'examines the remarkable achievements of a country now at a crossroads and facing up to the problems of its own success'. Cf. *also* The Study on Botswana by the U.N., 1987.

40. e.g. the statement by Canon Burgess Carr, General Secretary of the All Africa Conference of Churches, that God has 'sanctified violence into a redemptive instrument for bringing into being a fuller human life' (*op. cit.*, Chapter 6, Note 36 *above*). *See also* Appendix: **(iii)** Missionary Societies; **(iv)**, **(xxi)** *and* **(xxvi)** World Council of Churches; **(xi)** the Lambeth Conference, 1988; **(xiii)** Christian Aid; **(xviii)** *The Road to Damascus - Kairos and Conversion*, a document published by Christian Aid and the Catholic Institute for International Relations; **(xx)** SWAPO and the British Council of Churches; *see also*, for World Council of Churches activities, Part I, Chapter 6, *esp.* Notes 21 *and* 22.

41. *St Francis of Assisi* (London, Hodder & Stoughton, 1960 [1923]); p. 179.

42. The Church as the body of faithful believers is 'invisible' in the sense that her precise identity or extent is known only to God, as Wyclif asserted. This is because inward faith, as well as outward profession, is an essential requirement for membership, and the genuineness of another's faith (like the sincerity of another's motives) cannot be known with certainty by anyone. The corollary of this fact is Luther's argument, crucial to his protest as we have seen, that the true Church cannot be identified with any visible institution.

   The highly visible institutions called churches in the world of today contain spurious elements, as such institutions have always done. One of Jesus' parables (Mt 13:24-30) seems to picture such a situation, and other New Testament passages are explicit on the subject (Galat. 2:4; I Tim. 4:1-3; II Tim. 3:1-9; James 1:26; II Peter 2:1-3:7; I John 2:18-20; II John 2:7-9; Jude 3-19; Rev. 2:20-24; 3:1b-3; 14-19).

   None of which means that the true Church, though imprecisely identifiable, is unable to manifest her presence in the world. On the contrary, faithful individuals are 'the light of the world'. Dietrich Bonhoeffer, in his classic study *The Cost of Discipleship* (London, S.C.M., 1959 edition), is at pains to emphasize this. The discipleship of Jesus' followers, he writes (p. 106), is 'visible in action . . . the following is as visible to the world as a light in the darkness . . .'.

43. Mt 28:19, 20; Mk 16:15; Lk 24:46-48 *and* Acts 1:8.

44. Cf. Bready, J.W., *op. cit.*; *and* Schmidt, Sir Isaac, *The Social Results of Early Christianity* (London, Pitman, 1907).

45. *Bulletin of the Christian Institute for the Study of Religion and Society*, Bangalore, April 1961, p. 39.

Appendixes

The facts cited here illustrate further the political involvement of the churches, or the prevailing attitude among Christians that they should be politically involved, over the last two decades or so.

(i) The Revd Stanley Booth-Clibborn, at that time Vicar of Great St Mary's, Cambridge (now Bishop of Manchester), made the following points in the Annual Sermon of the Church Missionary Society, 1973: 'What once was fanciful and utopian is becoming a necessity if man is to survive ... so this element in the Gospel is coming to the fore once more - the challenge to a radical reshaping of economic life ... Our churches must give far more attention to economic and social equality in their normal programme of teaching and preaching ... The churches have been too afraid of being committed politically ... if social equality with a radical distribution of wealth is a Christian aim, we should back without reserve the points in political programmes which stand for these things ... the churches have a big part to play.' (See the sermon as published under the title *The End of the Monopoly Game: Christ's call to the Family of Man*, London, C.M.S., 1973, pp. 10-12).

(ii) *Christians in a Multiracial World*, a course of study prepared in 1973 by the British Council of Churches' Community and Race Relations Unit, in co-operation with the Church Missionary Society, London, quotes the Catholic Archbishop Helder Camara of Brazil (p. 10), who questions the condemnation of violence, commends (p. 11) the study of a leaflet about the World Council of Churches' (W.C.C.) Programme to Combat Racism, and recommends 'dialogue' (p. 14) as the Christian approach to other faiths. It also advertises (p. 18) the 'World Development Movement'.

In October 1973, incumbents of Anglican parishes received a circular from the General Synod of the Church of England which urged the claim of the World Development Movement, the manifesto of which, and an accompanying leaflet, *Europe '73 Programme*, were enclosed; each incumbent and his parishioners were invited to 'HELP TURN EUROPE INSIDE OUT'. (See *Church Times*, 12 October 1973).

(iii) The preacher for the Church Missionary Society in 1975 was the Revd Colin Morris, then President of the Methodist Missionary Society (later President of the Methodist Conference). In his book *Unyoung, Uncoloured, Unpoor* (London, Epworth, 1969), Morris argues the case, following S.G.F. Brandon (1967), for Jesus having been in sympathy with the first century AD Jewish Zealot movement and having made a bid for political leadership (pp. 100-21). Morris concludes (p. 122): 'Being prepared to believe that Jesus was involved in seditious activity against Rome, I must battle as best I can with the implications of that assumption.' Colin Morris is, in effect, an exponent of 'Liberation Theology' (cf. Chapter 6, Note 37, *above*).

(iv) Human rights is a prime concern of the modern Church, as Edward Norman (op. cit., p. 29-42), has pointed out. In an article, 'Churches' crisis of cash and Marxism' (*The Sunday Telegraph*, 23 November 1975), Christopher Dobson recorded that the 'work book' prepared for the delegates to the W.C.C. Fifth Assembly in Nairobi, 1975, declared that 'international monetary, trade and natural resource control systems are responsible for massive violation of human rights'; the article also recorded that by that date, besides the £128,000 allocated by the W.C.C. to liberation movements in 1975, the W.C.C. had paid out £12,500 to the London magazine *Race Today*, a magazine describing itself as dedicated to Black Power and the overthrow of the capitalist system.

(v) The Roman Catholic Church has moved in much the same direction as the Protestants on the issue of human rights.

The Second Vatican Council of 1965 was a watershed in Catholic attitudes on social and political issues, Edward Norman has argued, citing one of its documents (*Gaudium et Spes. Pastoral Constitution on the Church in the World Today*, London, Catholic Truth Society, 1966, p. 41; *see* Norman, *op. cit.*, p. 32): 'The Church, by virtue of the Gospel entrusted to her, proclaims men's rights and acknowledges and esteems the modern movement to promote these rights everywhere.' The Council was followed by Pope Paul VI's 1967 Encyclical, *Populorum Progressio*, which called for 'bold transformations' to redistribute the world's wealth, and questioned the validity of some of the basic tenets of capitalism - the profit motive, competition, and private ownership. 'Capitalism,' the Encyclical asserted, 'has been the cause of excessive suffering, injustices, and fratricidal conflicts whose effects still persist.' (*Pop. Prog.*, 26). And again: 'The rule of free trade, taken by itself, is no longer able to govern international relations ... It is the fundamental principle of liberalism [i.e. capitalism], as a rule for commercial exchange, which is questioned here.' (*Pop. Prog.*, 57, 58).

In 1968 the Latin American bishops met for the Medellín Conference, which declared that the Church's task was that of 'conscientizacion' - making the poor aware of their situation and of their rights: 'The Church - the People of God - will lend its support to the downtrodden of every social class so that they might come to know their rights and how to make use of them.' (Medellín Documents: Justice, 20) 'The Latin American Church has a message for all men on this continent who "hunger and thirst after justice" ... God ... sends his Son in the flesh ... to liberate all men from . . . hunger, misery, oppression and ignorance . . .' (Medellín Documents: Justice, 2, 3).

In 1971, Pope Paul VI's Pontifical letter, *Octogesima Adveniens*, addressed itself to 'the fairness in the exchange of goods and in the division of wealth between individuals and countries.' (*Oct. Adv.*, 7). The letter identified four levels of Marxism. While warning against the dangers of a totalitarian and violent society, the letter allowed that level four, a rigorous method of examining social and political reality and the practice of revolutionary transformation, was open for consideration by the Christian, and it referred to the erroneous affirmation of individual freedom which was the ideology underlying liberal capitalism (*Oct. Adv.*, 31-35).

On visiting Mexico in 1979, Pope John Paul II addressed the Oaxaca and Chiapas Indians. Departing from his prepared text, he said: 'I would like to reiterate ... that the present Pope wishes to be [quoting Paul VI] "in solidarity with your cause, which is the cause of humble people, the poor people" . . . the Pope is with the masses of people who are "almost always left behind in an ignoble standard of living and sometimes harshly treated and exploited" . . . I adopt the view of my predecessors, John XXIII and Paul VI, and of Vatican II . . . the Pope chooses to be your voice . . . He wishes to be the conscience of consciences; an invitation to action, to make up for lost time . . .' (See *The Bible, the Church, and Social Justice*, Richard Schiblin, Liguori, Mo., Liguori Publications, 1983, pp. 37, 38).

Pope John Paul II began his pontificate with a letter entitled *Redemptor Hominis* (1979). His concern was the inequitable distribution of goods in the world, largely arising from the domination of the poor by 'privileged social classes' and 'rich countries', the problem being so widespread 'that it brings into question the financial, monetary production and commercial mechanisms that, resting on various political pressures, support the world economy.' (*Red. Hom.*, 16). The letter also pointed to the evil of 'totalitarianisms'. (*Red. Hom.*, 17).

In 1981 Pope John Paul published *On Human Work*, a letter enunciating the principle of 'the priority of labour over capital', and arguing that both capitalism and Communism had produced an improper 'separation of labour and capital.' (*On H.W.*, 12, 13). Marxist collectivism, it stated, denies private ownership altogether; capitalism has forgotten that (as 'Christian tradition' asserts) 'the right to private property is subordinated to the right to common use.' To change the *status quo* Pope John Paul called for a new 'socialization' of the means of production by which the workers would come to control capital (*On H.W.*, 13, 14). There are clear Polish overtones to the letter: 'There is a need,' we read, 'for ever new movements of solidarity of the workers and with the workers.' (*On H.W.*, 8). More recently, *Laborem Exercens*, concerned with the creation and distribution of wealth, has taken some of the arguments a stage further.

The most recent encyclical, *Centesimus annus*, which marked the anniversary of Pope Leo XIII's revolutionary encyclical *Rerum Novarum* (the first of the long series of papal teachings on human rights in the light of economic developments), was issued on 2 May 1991. Underpinning the 30,000 word document is the church's conviction that it has a right to comment on social issues, structures and activities of mankind. It is concerned with poverty and human rights in a capitalist world. It declares that the rights of workers 'must be affirmed once more in the face of the changes we are witnessing', and identifies the violation of these rights as 'the decisive factor' in the fall of Communism in Eastern Europe; it criticizes the free-market society for excluding spiritual values much as Marxism did, and calls for 'the necessary intervention by public authorities' to prevent spiritual desertification; it also calls for a repudiation of the logic underlying war and for a funding of world economic development through savings made on disarmament programmes, urging the West to work towards rebuilding the states newly emerged from repression, without neglecting the Third World; and it emphasizes the need for the dissemination of know-how, technology and skill, enabling people to gain a fair access to the international market. (See *The Times*, 3 May 1991).

With regard to the implementation of Catholic social teaching, and the active involvement of the Church in the process, words written by Clifford Longley in *The Times*, 7 October 1989, sum up the situation: 'They [the social encyclicals] are the firm theoretical bedrock . . . beneath the Solidarity movement in Poland . . . The Christian Democrats in the European Parliament . . . have the social encyclicals as a key element in their basic philosophy. And if anyone doubts that Catholic social teaching can influence continents they have only to look to South America, where the church is busy acting as midwife to fundamental political change.'

For the Vatican's current political activity in the diplomatic sphere, *see* (**xxiv**), *below*; for its efforts as peacemaker, *see* (**xxvi**), *below*.

(**vi**) In February 1976, the Church Information Office (C.I.O.) of the Church of England, published a pamphlet written for the Board for Social Responsibility entitled *The State of the Nation*, to be used as the basis for a debate in the General Synod. It was written on the assumption that the Church had a distinctive and significant contribution to make to the solution of Britain's economic and political problems; it advocated 'the right kind of unity for the right kind of growth'; the principle of unity should 'govern a Christian approach to economics and politics'. (See *Church Times*, 13 February 1976).

(**vii**) In 1977 the C.I.O. published a report entitled *Understanding Closed Shops: A Christian Enquiry into Compulsory Trade Union Membership*. Despite Article 20 of the 1948 Universal Declaration of Human Rights ('No one may be compelled to belong to an association') quoted in its Chapter 4, the report argued (p. 22) that such 'general statements of principle' should be 'held in proper balance' and that certain factors in the situation could be held to 'outweigh the freedom not to belong to an association in certain cases'.

(**viii**) In 1979 the preacher for the Church Missionary Society Annual Sermon was the Right Revd Lakshman Wickremesinghe, Bishop of Kurunagela, Sri Lanka. His sermon was entitled *Mission, politics and evangelism*. 'Politics', he declared, 'as much as evangelism has always been a dimension of the mission of the church in the world. In our era we have become more self-conscious of the political dimension . . . Politics and evangelism are strange bed-fellows, but whom God has joined together the church must not put asunder.' (*See* p. 3 in the sermon as published by the C.M.S., London).

(**ix**) A body which, in the 1980s, fostered increasing political involvement by the Church of England in the sphere of race relations was the Race, Pluralism and Community Group of the Board for Social Responsibility of the Church of England. From 1 March 1985, it began publishing a series of occasional papers (edited by the Revd Ken Leech, the B.S.R.'s Race Relations Field Officer) entitled *Theology and Racism*, which examined some of the issues on which such action might be taken. (See *Church Times*, 1 March 1985).

(**x**) In 1985 a group in South Africa who called themselves 'The Kairos Theologians' produced *The Kairos Document: Challenge to the Church*, published in Braamfontein. The document, which refers frequently to the situation of the ancient Israelites, argues that Christians 'are supposed to do away with . . . injustice, oppression', and that the church in South Africa, which needs a 'political strategy', should 'participate in the struggle for liberation and a just society' (which might involve 'the use of physical force') by preaching about 'the *moral duty* . . . of all who are oppressed to resist oppression', by reshaping its 'services and sacraments . . . to further the liberating mission of God and the Church', and by encouraging, supporting and involving itself in 'the campaigns of the people'. (*See* Villa-Vicencio, C., *op. cit.*, pp. 251-69).

In July of the following year, the General Synod of the Church of England voted in favour of a resolution calling for economic sanctions against South Africa. (See *Church Times* for 11 & 17 July 1986).

For a detailed study of how in recent years the Church and church organizations have involved themselves in the often violent political struggles within South Africa, *see* Rachel Tingle's *Revolution of Reconciliation? The Struggle in the Church in South Africa* (London, Christian Studies Centre, 1992).

(**xi**) At the Lambeth Conference of Anglican bishops in 1988, in the Christianity and Social Order section of the Conference, a resolution was passed under the title 'War, Violence and Justice'. The wording of the resulution begs many questions. It says that the Conference:

'1a. Reaffirms the statement of the 1930 Lambeth Conference that war as a method of settling international disputes is incompatible with the teaching and example of our Lord Jesus Christ;

'b. Affirms also that there is no peace without justice, and that the overthrow of unjust systems and powers is a gospel imperative;

'2a. Supports those who choose the way of non-violence as being the way of our Lord including direct non-violent action, civil disobedience and conscientious objection, and pays tribute to those who in recent years have kept before the world the growing threat of militarism;

'b. Understands those who, after exhausting all other ways, choose the way of armed struggle as the only way to justice whilst drawing attention to the dangers and injustices possible in such action;

'3. Encourages provinces and dioceses to seek out those secular and religious agencies working for justice and reconciliation, and to make common cause with them, to ensure that the voice of the oppressed is heard and a response is made so that further violence is averted.' (see *The Daily Telegraph*, 5 August 1988).

The day following the passing of the resolution, on 5 August 1988, the bishops issued a statement to the effect that armed struggle was still wrong in Northern Ireland; if carried out in South Africa, apparently, it was not to be condemned. (See *The Sunday Telegraph*, 7 August 1988).

(**xii**) For the two years up to January, 1989, a Sri Lankan illegal immigrant, Viraj Mendis, was given sanctuary in a Manchester Church, a deportation order having been served on him in August 1985. On 20 January 1989, the police raided the church, where Mr Mendis had locked himself into his room and handcuffed himself to a radiator, and arrested him. The Bishop of Manchester, the Right Revd S. Booth-Clibborn (*see* Appendix (**i**)), 'deeply regretted' the action, and the Archbishop of Canterbury later described as 'regrettable' the Home Secretary's decision to use force. (See *Church Times*, 20 & 27 January 1989).

(**xiii**) In January 1989, Christian Aid, the official 'aid agency' of the British Council of Churches, did not deny that it had used its relief funds to support the Tanzanian 'Freedom College' of the African National Congress. The charge was made against it in a letter by Andrew V.R. Smith, of Western Goals UK, on 1 January 1989, in *The Sunday Telegraph* (following up more general charges made in the editorial of 18 December 1988) that by so doing it was helping to finance terrorism. The Chairman of Christian Aid, Sir Brian Young, pointed out in a letter of 22 January 1989, that the support took the form of medicines for the college's hospital. In his letter of 1 January, Mr Smith also emphasized that in 1988 Christian Aid had distributed a letter nationwide (*South Africa - Challenging Questions*) which included 'a justification of the ANC's savage necklace killings, comparing these hideously barbaric acts with the killings of Nazi collaborators in wartime Europe'. In a subsequent letter (15 January), Mr Smith drew attention to the fact that, in March 1988, Christian Aid had sponsored the Central American Week '88 campaign and encouraged anti-American 'vigils' at air force bases in Britain.

(xiv) From February 1989, the BBC ran a Lent series entitled *Sword and Spirit: the Local Church Responds*. Most church denominations in Britain recommended the series and its Group Study Notes, published by Marshall-Pickering [London] in 1988. Much of the emphasis of the programmes was on the need for the political liberation of the oppressed, and the comments of Charles Elliott, the producer, seemed to assume the desirability of a political interpretation of the Gospel (cf. 'liberation theology', mentioned on p. 16 of the Study Notes; for 'liberation theology' *see* Part I, Chapter 6, Note 37); the programmes on Brazil, Poland and the United States were especially politically orientated.

(xv) In March 1989, the Church of England effectively became an arm of government in the sphere of the creation of jobs; in that month the General Synod's Board of Social Responsibility accepted Government funding for a £430,000 initiative designed to aid inner-city regeneration. The project grew out of the Church's *Faith in the City* report, published in December 1985. In its consideration of the report the Board's Industrial and Economic Affairs Committee decided to look for ways to regenerate the local economy in urban priority areas. Jointly organizing the project was the body called Church Action with the Unemployed. The Church Urban Fund provided a further £21,000 for the project. (See *Church Times*, 23 March 1989).

(xvi) Also in March 1989, the Evangelical Alliance and the West Indian Evangelical Alliance became involved in job-creation schemes. They received £130,000 under the Home Office's 'Safer Cities Scheme' to fund two community workers under the 'Evangelical Enterprise' heading - an initiative started by the two Alliances in 1987 to encourage churches to help establish job-creation programmes. A spokesman for the Evangelical Alliance said that their motivation had been the 'biblical mandate to care for people in our communities'. (See *Church Times*, 17 March 1989).

(xvii) On 24 June 1989, in Leicester, the Revd Dr John Vincent chose his inaugural address as the President of the Methodist Conference to declare that the 'current policies' of the British government were a 'perversion' of Christian doctrine. Asserting that Christianity required human communities to hold as much as possible in common, Dr Vincent complained that privatization of much previously held by the State went in the opposite direction. (See *Church Times*, 30 June 1989).

(**xviii**) A document entitled *The Road to Damascus - Kairos and Conversion*, published by Christian Aid and the Catholic Institute for International Relations in August 1989, and signed by thousands of Christians world-wide, called for the 'conversion' of all 'right-wing' Christians and 'fundamentalists' (whom it described as 'heretics', and accused of 'the sins of idolatry, blasphemy, hypocrisy and even at times apostasy'). Such Christians, the document argued, should join those others who already supported those 'involved in struggles for national liberation'. (See *Church Times*, 8 August 1989).

(**xix**) By September 1989 all the major denominations in Britain had joined a new organization, the 'Southern Africa Coalition', the aim of which was to lobby for effective sanctions against South Africa. The organization included such bodies as Friends of the Earth and the Inland Revenue Staff Federation. The participation of the General Synod of the Church of England was decided by the International Affairs Committee of the Board for Social Responsibility. The Coalition grew out of a conference on Britain and Southern Africa organized by the British Council of Churches and Christian Aid in February 1989. (See *Church Times*, 8 September 1989).

(**xx**) A report, *No Escape from Misery*, published in September 1989 by the International Society for Human Rights, alleged widespread torture and executions of prisoners by the South West Africa Peoples' Organization (SWAPO) in Angola. It claimed that churches in the region had played an active part in the campaign to conceal SWAPO's violation of human rights. In a letter to the British Council of Churches, the Secretary General of the Society's British Section, Robert Chambers, described the 'uncritical solidarity' of British Churches with SWAPO as 'shameful'. The General Secretary of the B.C.C., Dr Philip Morgan, stated: 'We will respond, but not with enormous urgency . . .' (See *Church Times*, 15 September 1989).

(**xxi**) The World Council of Churches announced, in September 1989, that its Special Fund to Combat Racism was awarding grants for the current year totalling £309,000; by far the largest proportion of the grants was going to groups in Southern Africa, including a grant of £103,000 to SWAPO. The President of the W.C.C., responding to allegations of torture and detention of Namibians by SWAPO officials, stated that he was 'deeply saddened', but that 'our support for SWAPO was on the understanding shared by the international community that SWAPO represented the aspirations of the people of Namibia. The Churches in Namibia have, of course, been part of that movement for liberation and justice in Namibia . . . We have pledged ourselves to maintain a critical solidarity with the people of Namibia and SWAPO.' He pointed out that the terms of the Special Fund state that no check is made on how the grant is spent 'as an expression of the commitment by the PCR [Programme to Combat Racism] to the cause of economic, social and political justice'. (See *Church Times*, 29 September 1989).

(xxii) In the autumn of 1989, East German church buildings became the rallying point for a political organization, 'New Forum', whose aim was to press the government for reforms, and church leaders became spokesmen for this 'nascent political opposition'. (See *Financial Times*, 23 October 1989: 'Austere Berlin Church is rallying point for reformers'; *The Independent*, 20 October 1989: 'East Germans sceptical as Krenz talks to Church'); cf. the article by Paul Oestreicher in *Church Times*, 3 November 1989, 'The Courageous Church that is helping a new East Germany to birth', in which (ironically) he declared that the East German church's political involvement was carrying on the 'tradition of Luther's Reformation'; cf. *also* the article 'Every hand and every thought is needed here - Church action in East Germany: eye-witness report by Humphrey Fisher', in *Church Times*, 24 November 1989.

(xxiii) On 4 December 1989, the ecumenical pressure group Church Action on Poverty, launched its manifesto in Westminster Abbey, London. The *Church Times* reported (8 December 1989): 'Church Action on Poverty deplores a wide range of the manifestations of poverty and Government policies which, it believes, exacerbate them. The manifesto thus criticizes the number of people without jobs or homes, the discrepancy between the rich and the poor, and the decay of the National Health Service and state education. It also challenges curbs on trade union power and restrictions on press and broadcasting.' One of the speakers at the launch, Fr. Michael Campbell-Johnson, the UK Provincial of the the Jesuits, declared: 'This is not a party political statement . . . we are on the side of the poor.' Another speaker, Bishop Trevor Huddleston, called implicitly for political demonstrations: 'I pray for the day,' he said, 'when it is not Tiananmen Square or Wenceslaus Square but when it is Trafalgar Square which is filled with thousands saying "this must stop" '. By 8 December 1989, a hundred church leaders had signed the manifesto, including several Anglican bishops, the Roman Catholic Bishop of Liverpool, and the Presidents of the Methodist Conference and the Baptist Union. (See *Church Times*, 24 November & 8 December 1989).

(xxiv) The political character of the Roman Catholic Church, with its diplomatic missions spread around the world, was highlighted at the end of 1989. General Manuel Noriega of Panama, ousted on 20 December from his position as dictator by invading US forces, surrendered on Christmas Eve, but did so at the Vatican embassy, where he obtained asylum. The United States had, in the words of President Bush, intervened in Panama to restore democracy; to protect the Panama Canal; to safeguard American lives in Panama, and to bring General Noriega to justice [he was wanted in the United States on charges of drugs trafficking and racketeering]. On 29 December 1989, the Vatican denounced the United States as an 'occupying force' in Panama, saying that President Bush had no right to demand the handover of Noriega from the Papal Nunciature in Panama City. (See *The Times*, 21 & 17 December 1989, and *The Daily Telegraph*, 30 December 1989).

There has in general been a high profile in recent years for the problems faced by the Vatican operating as a political entity. Controversy has, for instance, surrounded Pope John Paul's readiness officially to receive at the Vatican the PLO leader Yasser Arafat in 1982 (and again in 1988), as also the question of Papal diplomatic recognition, or otherwise, of the State of Israel - though on the latter issue progress seems to be speeding up with the creation by the Vatican and Israel, in July 1992, of a permanent joint commission to study subjects of mutual interest, the aim being, according to the chief Vatican spokesman, Mr Navarro-Valls, 'a normalization of relations'. (See *The Times*, 30 July 1992; *also* letter to *The Times*, 4 August 1992, from Mr Israel Finestein, President of the Board of Deputies of British Jews).

The diplomatic problem constituted by Israel is, however, only one among many such problems; for as the 1990s progress following the collapse of Communism world-wide and the fragmentation of the Soviet Union into independent states, the decision whether or not to exchange ambassadors with some newly emerged sovereign body is seldom off the Vatican agenda.

The current Papal policy seems to be to make a virtue of necessity. There are signs of a new Papal *Europapolitik*. The old *Ostpolitik*, denoting the Vatican's political relations with Eastern Europe, is likely to be subsumed under a grand design for the Catholic conquest of both Eastern and Western Europe. (See *The Independent*, 16 August 1991, 'Rome's Eastern Block', by Peter Hebblethwaite) 'It is in the movement towards federalism of the Common Market, with the coming membership of Eastern European countries, as well as in the turmoil in the Soviet Union, that the Pope may see the greatest possibility for an increase in Catholic political power since the fall of Napoleon, or since the Counter-Reformation.' (See *The Sunday Telegraph*, 25 August 1991, 'Now, a Holy Roman Empire?' - a profile on Pope John Paul II, whom the article describes as 'the most political Pope of modern times'). A meeting of all European bishops was called by Pope John Paul for the end of November 1991, in order to discuss the Vatican's new European strategy; meanwhile the work has already begun with the Vatican's diplomatic service 'opening Papal nunciatures in Eastern Europe at a faster rate than McDonald's'. (See *The Sunday Telegraph*, 21 July 1991, 'Hatching a New Popish Plot', by William Ward). The old Vatican view that the temporal power of the Church is necessary for the furtherance of her spiritual work is clearly far from dead. (Cf. Chapter 6, under *Ecclesiastical retrenchment and theological conflict*).

For a detailed study of the Vatican's enhanced political stance under Pope John Paul II, *see* David Willey's account in *God's Politician: John Paul at the Vatican* (London, Faber, 1992). David Willey concludes the book (p. 239): 'The most positive and enduring legacy of John Paul will be the Vatican's renewed international political role and the Pope's claim to the ethical leadership of an increasingly secularized world society.'

(**xxv**) Anglican Church leaders have in recent years been very ready to condemn groups of people who may not, and sometimes certainly do not, have any church affiliation, as the following examples illustrate:

(a) In 1989 Dr Runcie, Archbishop of Canterbury [now Lord Runcie], in an interview published in the October issue of the magazine *Director*, questioned some of the basic tenets of 'Thatcherism', which he said was leading to a 'Pharisee' society. He implied that 'our political and commercial leadership' was guilty of Pharisaical 'self-righteousness' and 'judgmental attitudes' - a curious charge, since these are usually the sins of those with strong religious pretensions, such as the religious leaders (the Pharisees) of first century Judaism. The irony of his position

- that he was himself a religious leader sitting in judgement on a group of people many of whom would have made no Christian profession - seems entirely to have escaped Dr Runcie.

Jesus, by contrast, did not condemn the political establishment of his day (the Romans; cf. John 19:11), nor those who made money (cf. Lk 19:1-10). In fact he condemned no one, except those who, like the Pharisees, were convinced that they were beyond reproach. He recognized the sin that was common to man, and he taught that all men would perish because of it if they did not repent (Lk 13:1-5); but he did not condemn the sinner (Jn 8:11).

(b) On Christmas Eve, 1989, Archbishop Desmond Tutu made the extraordinary statement to 'a large crowd of Palestinians' near Bethlehem that 'God is on your side'. (See *Church Times*, 5 January 1990). In so saying he immediately compromised the efforts of those seeking to bring the message of God's love in Christ to Jewish Israelis by implying that God had somehow aligned himself *against* the latter. Significantly, Muslims understood some other of Archbishop Tutu's words during that visit ('unjust governments will bite the dust') as indicating his support, and presumably a degree of church support, for the political aspirations of Palestinians, since the Islamic Propagation Centre International (IPCI) 'publicly congratulated the Archbishop' on his criticism of the Israeli Government in relation to its policy for Palestine. (See *Al-Burhan: the voice of the IPCI*, Vol. I, No. 10, June 1990, p. 2).

(c) In July 1991, the General Synod of the Church of England called for a boycott of *Nescafé* coffee in protest at the distribution of free breast milk substitutes in the Third World by its manufacturer, Nestlé. (See *The Daily Telegraph*, 17 July 1991: 'Synod backs Nescafé ban'). In a letter to *The Times* (18 July 1991), Mr Peter Blackburn, Chairman and Managing Director of Nestlé UK, rebutted the charge of unethical conduct by his company, and concluded: 'I resent the attack on the moral integrity of our company and its 20,000 UK employees'.

Two days later (as reported by *The Sunday Times*, 21 July 1991) it was made public that the Church of England had earned £80,000 in dividends from a £1,400,000 investment in Nestlé.

(d) In a sermon that formed part of a (question-begging) service held in Derby Cathedral on 10 May 1992, to give thanks to God for the single European market, Dr Carey, Archbishop of Canterbury, attacked greed among industrialists, suggested that God would curse those who waited for the 'trickle-down effect' to feed the poor, and argued that the purpose of trade and industry was 'not to make profits for shareholders, nor to create salaries and wages for the industrial community', but to 'serve people by creating things of use and value to them'. The sermon drew protests for its judgemental attitude towards businessmen from several Conservative MPs, and specific refutation from the Director General of the Institute of Directors, Mr Peter Morgan, who said: 'Dr Carey's remarks appear to demonstrate a fundamental misunderstanding of the dynamism of the market economy'. (See *The Independent*, 11 May 1992: 'Archbishop condemns big pay rises', by Andrew Brown; also *The Daily Telegraph*, 12 May 1992).

In a follow-up letter to *The Independent*, 12 May 1992), Mr Morgan quoted some words of Adam Smith: 'It is not from the benevolence of the butcher, the brewer and the baker that we expect our dinner, but from their regard to their own interest'. He commented further: 'The virtue of the market is that it provides the opportunity for people to promote the general good, while at the same time acting in their own self-interest - Adam Smith's "invisible hand".'

(xxvi) The Gulf war of January/February 1991, and the issue of an overall Middle East peace settlement, have highlighted a current activity of the Church which the large majority of Christians assume to be axiomatic to her role - the work of peacemaking in the political sphere. This is often, of course, merely seen as a part of the wider political work claimed for the Church, that of furthering social justice and promoting human rights. (Cf., *inter alia*, Wright, T., *New Tasks for a Renewed Church*, London, Hodder & Stoughton, 1992, pp. 109, 110, 129, 161-9).

From 7 to 20 February 1991, at the height of the Gulf war, the Seventh Assembly of the World Council of Churches was held in Canberra, Australia. At its conclusion the Assembly called for an immediate and unconditional ceasefire in the war, as well as for the convening of an International Peace Conference on the Middle East to address the legitimate rights of Palestinians to an independent state of their own and to implement the UN Security Council Resolution 242 (1967). (*See* the Assembly's resolutions under 'Appeals and Affirmations', Clauses 39 and 40; see also *The Times*, 19 February 1991, 'Churches call for a ceasefire').

Pope John Paul adopted a broadly pacifist and non-aligned stance during the conflict. This was reflected firstly in his affirmation, at the Extraordinary Summit of Catholic patriarchs and bishops from countries involved in the Gulf war held in the Vatican, 4 & 5 March 1991, that for years already war had been excluded as a means of solving conflicts between nations (see *MECC Newsreport*, March 1991), and secondly in a leading article in the Jesuit magazine *La Civilitá Cattolica* that bewails the death and destruction caused by the Allied attack and declares the theory of a 'just war' to be outdated. (See *The Sunday Telegraph*, 21 July 1991, 'Gulf war through Jesuit eyes'). The Pope's efforts during the Gulf conflict to secure peace and promote reconciliation were in fact saluted in a letter sent to him by the Secretary-General of the Islamic Conference. (See *MECC Newsreport*, March 1991).

At the above Extraordinary Summit held in the Vatican it was also affirmed that the primary orientations for the Catholic Church in its work in the Middle East included the need to find solutions for the Palestinian problem, the situation in Lebanon, and the Kurdish and Cypriot problems, the need to control the arms trade, and the need for a resolution of economic inequalities.

In similar vein, a week-long meeting of the Primates of the Anglican Communion, under the chairmanship of the newly appointed Archbishop of Canterbury, Dr George Carey, held in Newcastle, Northern Ireland, concluded on 13 April 1991 with a re-affirmation of the resolution passed at the 1988 Lambeth Conference on the West Bank and Gaza. The resolution affirms the important role of the Church in promoting peace, justice and reconciliation, as well as recognizing both the existence of Israel and the rights of Palestinians to self-determination, expressing the Conference's support for the convening of an international conference under UN auspices to resolve the conflict, and calling for the United Nations to 'assume the administration of the West Bank and Gaza from the State of Israel . . . until there is a settlement of the Israeli-Palestinian issue'. (See *MECC Newsreport*, May 1991).

Nine months later, in January 1992, Dr Carey embarked on a kind of peace mission to the Middle East, visiting Amman and Jerusalem. In the course of his trip he met members of the Jordanian and Israeli governments and representatives of the Palestinian community. He declared that both Jews and Palestinians 'have a right to belong here, and each community should recognize that right in the other', and on meeting the Israeli Prime Minister, Yitzhak Shamir, he broached the question of Palestinian political and human rights, urging the Jewish state to remove obstacles to peace such as the proposed deportation of twelve Palestinian activists from the occupied territories. He later criticized the deportation orders as 'rough justice'. (See *The Times*, 6, 8 and 9 January 1992).

A Palestinian Christian's theological response to the Israeli-Palestinian issue is seen in the book *Justice, and only Justice*, by Naim Stifan Ateek (New York, Orbis Books, 1989). In it Father Ateek argues that the Church in Israel-Palestine has a dual ministry, 'a prophetic and a peacemaking one', denoting respectively 'the active promotion of justice' and working as 'a catalyst of peace and reconciliation' (pp. 151, 152). In fulfilment of this 'dual imperative' Father Ateek proposes that all the churches in Israel-Palestine should set up a 'Center for Peacemaking', the establishment of which he describes as 'the greatest calling of the Church in Israel-Palestine' (p. 158).

Father Ateek, a Roman Catholic, is not of course going beyond what his superior, Pope John Paul, stands for - as we have seen above, and as the latter's 1991 Christmas message underlines. According to press reports, the message was almost exclusively political. It was devoted to the problem of peace and justice between men and nations, with scarcely a nod in the direction of God, and not a word on the fundamental problem addressed by the incarnation - that of man's need for peace and reconciliation with his Maker, in order to restore the broken relationship and lift man from his natural state of depravity. (See *The Times*, 26 December 1991, 'The Pope calls for an end to hatred and war').

We can see how the belief in the Church's role as peacemaker has also impelled the churches and their leaders in other questionable directions. The work of negotiating the release of hostages pursued by Mr Terry Waite (until his own kidnapping in January 1987) can be seen as a form of peacemaking. Had Mr Waite been acting solely on his own behalf, or on behalf of an agency like Amnesty International, or on behalf of a government, no criticism could be made of his political missions as negotiator, with all that those missions entailed; but he was acting on behalf of the Church of England, designated as he was the 'Special Envoy' of the then Archbishop of Canterbury, Dr Runcie, and officially sent forth by him.

The urge to promote peace in wider society has likewise encouraged the churches to support not only inter-faith dialogue but also inter-faith worship and prayer. Dr Carey, for instance, has defended the holding of the inter-faith Commonwealth service in Westminster Abbey each spring on the ground that not to hold it would 'suggest to members of other faith communities that they were an unwelcome presence in our society'. (See *The Times*, 9 December 1991, 'Clergy rebel over multi-faith worship', by Ruth Gledhill). Pope John Paul, too, in his annual peace message of December 1991, has affirmed (in the spirit of his inter-faith pilgrimage to pray for world peace at Assisi in 1986) the need for acceptance of other faiths. (See *The Times* leader, 11 December 1991, 'Tolerating Christians').

Most worrying of all is the effective denial by church leaders on occasions, in the supposed interests of fostering peace in society, of the indispensability of the Church's evangelistic role. This, as the Revd Tony Higton has pointed out [letter to

The Times 17 March 1992], is the force of Dr Carey's decision not to accept an invitation - accepted by his predecessors for the past one hundred and fifty years - to become patron of the Anglican Church's Ministry Among the Jews, for whom evangelism among those of the Jewish faith is an unquestioned aim. As a leader in *The Times* put it (12 March 1992): 'With the Jewish community in Britain becoming increasingly sensitive about Christian proselytism in its ranks, his acceptance would be hard to square with his joint presidency of the Council of Christians and Jews.' Cf. Coughlin, C., *Hostage: The Complete Story of the Lebanon Captives* (London, Little, Brown, 1992).

Whatever the intentions of all these efforts by the Church at being peacemaker in the world at large, as in working more generally for socio-political justice, the fact remains that they inevitably involve her (at the very least) in making moral judgements, and from time to time issuing condemnatory statements, about those who are not her own. This compromises the fulfilment of her one true and spiritual task in relation to the world - that of evangelism. (Cf. Appendix **(xxv)**, *above*).

'But surely', it is argued, 'Jesus himself said: "Blessed are the peacemakers."' (Mt 5:9). What he said about peace elsewhere, however, does not suggest that he was here referring to those who work for peace at the worldly, political level. Take some of his parting words to his disciples: 'Peace I leave with you; my peace I give to you; not as the world gives do I give to you.' (Jn 14:27). The peace Jesus was concerned about was not of this world, it was inner and spiritual; and it was surely those who work for that deeper peace whom he blessed, even calling them 'sons of God' - as he also blessed the poor 'in spirit', not necessarily the literally poor, and those who hunger and thirst 'after righteousness', not necessarily the literally hungry and thirsty (Mt 5:3, 6). As regards the peace of this world, Jesus said: 'Do you think that I have come to give peace on earth? No, I tell you, but rather division.' (Lk 12:51). By which he meant, as his further words on this and other occasions bear out, that his very message of spritual peace between man and God would sometimes cause dissension even between members of the same family. And of course for his followers he promised tribulation in this world, not an outwardly peaceful life (Jn 16:33).

It is doubtless still true that Christians should seek the worldly, outward kind of peace while this does not conflict with their prior loyalty to the truth. But this is no reason for the Church to take upon herself the role of the world's arbitrator, any more than Jesus agreed to arbitrate for the man who asked him to settle a problem of inheritance with his brother (Lk 12:13, 14). It is one thing for individual Christians to desire the peace of this world when appropriate, and pursue it when possible, perhaps working for it through a secular agency or government. It is quite another for the Church to go beyond the mandate given by Jesus, who refused to be a political figure of any description, whether this involved waging war or striving for peace, and whose example the Church (his body on earth) is supposed to follow.

Bibliography
(including Important Texts)

Acton (Lord Acton), *Lectures on Modern History*, London, Macmillan, 1906.

Archbishop of Canterbury's Commission on Urban Priority Areas, Report of, *Faith in the City*, London, Church House Publishing, 1985.

Ateek, N.S., *Justice and Only Justice: A Palestinian Theology of Liberation*, New York, Orbis, 1989.

Atīya, A., *Crusade, Commerce and Culture*, [Indiana University Press, 1962]; New York, John Wiley and Sons, Inc., Science Editions Paperback, 1966.

Anderson, D., 'Eating Sheppard's Pie: Hints on Reading the Sociological Gospel', in the Symposium (edited by him), *The Kindness that Kills*, London, SPCK, 1984.

Augustine, *The City of God*; abridged edn by Wand, J.C.W., London, Oxford University Press, 1963.

Barth, K., 'The Christian Community and the Civil Community' in *Against the Stream*, London, SCM, 1954.

Binyon, G.C., *The Christian Socialist Movement in England*, London, SPCK, 1931.

Boehmer, H., *Der Junge Luther*, Muhlenberg Press, 1946; English translation, *Martin Luther: Road to Reformation*, London, Thames & Hudson, 1957.

Bonhoeffer, D., *The Cost of Discipleship*, London, SCM, 1959 edn [1948].

————, *Letters and Papers from Prison*, London, SCM, 1953.

Brandon, S.G.F., *The Fall of Jerusalem and the Christian Church*, London, SPCK, 1951.

————, *Jesus and the Zealots*, Manchester University Press, 1967.

————, *The Trial of Jesus of Nazareth*, London, Batsford, 1967.

Bready, J.W., *England: Before and After Wesley*, London, Hodder & Stoughton, 1938.

Bruce, F.F., *Are the New Testament Documents Reliable?*, London, IVF, 1943.

————, *The Spreading Flame*, Exeter, Paternoster, 1958.

Butterfield, H., *Christianity in European History*, London, Collins, 1952.

Campbell, J. McLeod, *Christian History in the Making*, London, Church Assembly Press and Publications Board, 1964.

Carmichael, J., *The Death of Jesus*, London, Gollancz, 1963.

Carmichael, J.D., and Goodwin, H.S., *William Temple's Political Legacy*, London, Mowbray, 1963.

Casey, M., *From Jewish Prophet to Gentile God*, Cambridge, James Clarke, 1991.

Catchpole, D.R., *The Trial of Jesus: A Study in the Gospels and Jewish Historiography from 1770 to the Present Day*, Leiden, E.J. Brill, 1971.

Chadwick, O., *The Reformation*, London, Penguin, 1964.

Chesterton, G.K., *St Francis of Assisi*, London, Hodder & Stoughton, 1923.

127

Cox, H., *The Secular City*, London, SCM, 1965.

Cragg, G.R., *The Church and the Age of Reason*, London, Penguin, 1960.

DeGrucy, J., and Villa-Vicencio, C. (eds), *Apartheid is a Heresy*, Cambridge, The Lutterworth Press, 1983.

Dodd, C.H., *The Founder of Christianity*, London, Collins, 1971.

Dorrien, G.J., *Reconstructing the Common Good: Theology and The Social Order*, New York, Orbis, 1990.

Eisler, R., *The Messiah Jesus and John the Baptist*, London, Methuen, 1931.

Elton, G.R., *Reformation Europe 1517-1559*, London, Collins (Fontana History of Europe), 1963.

Eusebius, *Ecclesiastical History*; see the Greek text, with transl. by Kirsopp Lake, Loeb Classical Library (2 vols), Harvard University Press, Mass./Heinemann, London, 1980 [First edition, 1926].

Ferguson, J., *The Politics of Love: The New Testament and Non-Violent Revolution*, Cambridge, James Clarke, 1973.

Fisher, H.A.L., *A History of Europe*, London, Eyre & Spottiswoode, 1935.

Fox, R.L., *Christians and Pagans in the Mediterranean world from the second century AD to the conversion of Constantine*, London, Penguin, 1988 [1986].

Furneaux, R., *The Empty Tomb*, London, Panther, 1963.

Grayzel, S., *A History of the Jews*, New York, Mentor, 1968 [1947].

Griffiths, B., *Morality and the Market Place*, London, Hodder & Stoughton, 1982.

Gutiérrez, G., *A Theology of Liberation. History, Politics and Salvation*, London, SCM, 1971.

Hamilton, K., *Earthly Good: the Churches and the Betterment of Human Existence*, Grand Rapids, Mich., Eerdmans, 1990.

Hill, C., *Intellectual Origins of the English Revolution* London, Panther, 1972 [OUP, 1965].

Horsley, R.A., with Hanson, J.S., *Bandits, Prophets, and Messiahs: Popular Movements in the Time of Jesus*, Winston Press, Minn., 1985; paperback edn, San Francisco, Harper & Row, 1988.

Huddleston, T., *Naught for Your Comfort*, London, Collins, 1956 (Fontana, 1957).

Jackson, F.J. Foakes, and Lake, K., *The Beginnings of Christianity*, London, Macmillan, 1920.

Jenkins, D., 'Doctrines Which Drive One to Politics', in the Symposium *Christian Faith and Political Hopes: A Reply to E.R. Norman*, London, Epworth, 1979.

————, *God, Politics and the Future*, London, SCM, 1988.

Jones, A.H.M., *Constantine and the Conversion of Europe*, London, Pelican, 1972 [EUP, 1949].

Josephus, *Antiquities of the Jews and Wars of the Jews*, translated by William Whiston, London, J.M. McGowan [no date].

Kahl, J., *The Misery of Christianity*, London, Penguin, 1971 [Hamburg, 1968].

Kairos Theologians, The, *The Kairos Document: Challenge to the Church*, Braamfontein, 1985.

Kierkegaard, S., *Journals*; see *The Journals of Kierkegaard, 1834-1854*, edited and translated by Alexander Dru, London, Fontana, 1958 [OUP, 1938].

King, M. Luther, *Strength to Love*, London, Fontana, 1969 [Hodder & Stoughton, 1964).

Lee, P., *Poor Man, Rich Man*, London, Hodder & Stoughton, 1986.

Lewis, C.S., *Mere Christianity*, London, Fontana, 1955 [Collins, 1952].

Lietzmann, H., *History of the Early Church* (4 vols, translated from the German by B.M. Woolf), London/Cambridge, The Lutterworth Press, 1949-51 [1937]; new paperback edn (2 vols), 1993.

Lindsay, A.D., *The Two Moralities: Our Duty to God and to Society*, London, Eyre & Spottiswoode, 1940.

Luther, Martin, *The Papacy at Rome; Open Letter to the Christian Nobility of the German Nation; The Babylonish Captivity of the Church; Concerning Christian Liberty; An Admonition to Peace; Secular Authority: to What Extent It Should Be Obeyed*; see *Works of Martin Luther*, Philadelphia, NJ., Muhlenberg Press, 1959; *see also* Porter, J.M., *op. cit.*

Martin, D.A., *Pacifism: An Historical and Sociological Study*, London, Routledge & Kegan Paul, 1965.

Mascall, E.L., *The Secularisation of Christianity*, London, Darton, Longman & Todd, 1965.

Maurice, F.D., *The Kingdom of Christ*, London, Macmillan, 1842.

Morison, F., *Who Moved the Stone?* London, Faber, 1930.

Morris, C., *Unyoung, Uncoloured, Unpoor*, London, Epworth, 1969.

Neill, S., *A History of Christian Missions*, London, Penguin, 1964.

Norman, E.R., *Christianity and the World Order*, London, Oxford University Press, 1979.

Oddie, W., 'Christian Socialism: An Old Heresy', in *The Kindness that Kills*, ed. by Anderson, D., London, SPCK, 1984.

Ozment, S., *The Age of Reform, 1250-1550*, London, Yale University Press, 1980.

Parker, G.H.W., *The Morning Star*, Exeter, Paternoster, 1965.

Perry, M.C., *The Easter Enigma*, London, Faber, 1959.

Porter, J.M., (ed.), *Luther: Selected Political Writings*, Philadelphia, NJ., Fortress Press, 1974.

Powell, J. Enoch, 'The Church and the Work of the World', in *No Easy Answers*, London, Sheldon, 1973.

Ramsay, A.M., *The Resurrection of Christ*, London, Bles, 1945.

Rauschenbusch, W., *Christianity and the Social Crisis*, New York, Hodder & Stoughton/Macmillan, 1907.

————, *Christianizing the Social Order*, New York, Macmillan, 1912.

————, *A Theology for the Social Gospel*, London, Macmillan, 1918 [New York, 1917].

Reardon, B.M., *Religious Thought in the Reformation*, London, Longman, 1981.

Richardson, A., *A Political Christ*, London, SCM, 1973.

Ritschl, A., (as translated by H.R. Mackintosh and A.B. Macaulay), *The Christian Doctrine of Justification and Reconciliation: The Positive Development of the Doctrine*, Reference Book Publishers, NJ., 1966 [Edinburgh, T & T Clarke, 1900; 1st edn 1874].

Robinson, J.A.T., *Redating the New Testament*, London, SCM, 1976.

Schiblin, R., *The Bible, The Church, and Social Justice*, Liguori, MO., Liguori Publications, 1983.

Schmidt, Sir Isaac, *The Social Results of Early Christianity*, London, Pitman, 1907.

Schonfield, H.J., *The Passover Plot*, London, Hutchinson, 1965.

————— , *Those Incredible Christians*, London, Hutchinson, 1968.

————— , *The Pentecost Revolution*, London, Macdonald, 1974.

Sheehan, T., *The First Coming: How the Kingdom of God Became Christianity*, New York, Vintage Books, 1988 [Random House, 1986].

Sheppard, D., *Built as a City*, London, Hodder & Stoughton, 1974.

————— , *Bias to the Poor*, London, Hodder & Stoughton, 1983.

Sheppard, D., and Worlock, D., *Better Together*, London, Penguin, 1989 [first published, without Postscript, by Hodder & Stoughton, 1988].

Sherrard, P., 'The Desanctification of Nature', in *Sanctity and Secularity: the Church and the World* ('Studies in Church History', Vol. 10, ed. by D. Baker), Oxford, Blackwell, 1973.

Sipendi, J., *The Arusha Declaration and Christian Socialism*, Dar es Salaam, 1969.

Social and Industrial Council of the Church Assembly, The, *The National Church and the Social Order*, London, Church Information Board, 1956.

Southern, R.W., *Western Society and the Church in the Middle Ages*, London, Pelican, 1970.

Sugden, C., *Social Gospel or No Gospel?*, Bramcote, Grove Books, 1975.

Temple, W., *Hope for the New World*, London, SCM, 1940.

————— , *Citizen and Churchman*, London, Eyre & Spottiswoode, 1941.

————— , *Christianity and Social Order*, London, Penguin, 1942.

Thiede, C., *Jesus: Life or Legend*, Oxford, Lion, 1990.

Tingle, R., *Revolution or Reconciliation? The Struggle in the Church in South Africa*, London, Christian Studies Centre, 1992.

Toynbee, A.J., *Survey of International Affairs*, London, Royal Institute of International Affairs, 1931.

————— , *A Study of History* (abridgement of volumes 1-6 by D.C. Somervell), London, Oxford University Press, 1946.

Villa-Vicencio, C., *Between Christ and Caesar: Classic and Contemporary Texts on Church and State*, Grand Rapids, Mich., Eerdmans, 1986.

Vidler, A.R., *The Church in an Age of Revolution*, London, Penguin, 1961.

Wenham, J.W., *Redating Matthew, Mark and Luke*, London, Hodder & Stoughton, 1991.

Westcott, B.F., *Social Aspects of Christianity*, London, Macmillan, 1887.

————— , *Lessons from Work*, London, Macmillan, 1901.

————— , *The Two Empires*, London, Macmillan, 1909.

Willey, D., *God's Politician: John Paul at the Vatican*, London, Faber, 1992.

Winter, P., *On the Trial of Jesus*, Berlin, de Gruyter, 1961.

Wright, T., *New Tasks for a Renewed Church*, London, Hodder & Stoughton, 1992.

Wyclif, John, *De Ecclesia*; see edn by J. Loserth, London, 1886.

Yoder, J.H., *The Politics of Jesus*, Grand Rapids, Mich., Eerdmans, 1972.

Index

131